AN

HISTORICAL ACCOUNT

OF THE

DOINGS AND SUFFERINGS

OF

THE CHRISTIAN INDIANS

IN NEW ENGLAND,

IN THE YEARS 1675, 1676, 1677

IMPARTIALLY DRAWN BY ONE WELL ACQUAINTED WITH THAT AFFAIR,

AND

PRESENTED UNTO THE RIGHT HONOURABLE

THE CORPORATION RESIDING IN LONDON, APPOINTED BY THE KING'S

MOST EXCELLENT MAJESTY FOR PROMOTING THE GOSPEL

AMONG THE INDIANS IN AMERICA.

Kessinger Publishing's Rare Reprints
Thousands of Scarce and Hard-to-Find Books!

We kindly invite you to view our extensive catalog list at:
http://www.kessinger.net

ARCHÆOLOGIA AMERICANA.

TRANSACTIONS

AND

COLLECTIONS

OF THE

AMERICAN ANTIQUARIAN SOCIETY.

VOLUME II.

CAMBRIDGE:
PRINTED FOR THE SOCIETY,
AT THE
UNIVERSITY PRESS.
1836.

The Erroneous Pagination Appears As It Was In The Original Book.

PRELIMINARY NOTICE.

In preparing the following brief sketch of the principal incidents in the life of the author of " The History of the Christian Indians," the Publishing Committee have consulted the original authorities cited by the American biographical writers, and such other sources of information as were known to them, for the purpose of insuring greater accuracy; but the account is almost wholly confined to the period of his residence in New England, and is necessarily given in the most concise manner. They trust, that more ample justice will yet be done to his memory by the biographer and the historian.

DANIEL GOOKIN was born in England, about A. D. 1612. As he is termed " a Kentish soldier " by one of his contemporaries, who was himself from the County of Kent,* it has been inferred, with good reason, that Gookin was a native of that county. In what year he emigrated to America, does not clearly appear; but he is supposed to have first settled in the southern colony of Virginia, from whence he removed to New England. Cotton Mather, in his memoir of Thompson, a nonconformist divine of Virginia, has the following quaint allusion to our author:

> " A constellation of great converts there
> Shone round him, and his heavenly glory were.
> GOOKINS was one of these. By Thompson's pains,
> Christ and New England a dear Gookins gains."

A gentleman of the same name, " Master Daniel Gookin," (as he is styled,) accompanied by " fifty men of his own, and thirty passengers, well provided, arrived out of Ireland," in Virginia, Nov. 22d, 1621. He was one of twenty-six persons, to whom patents of lands were granted in that year, and who are said to " have undertaken to transport great multitudes of people and cattle to Virginia."† Having fulfilled his contract with the Virginia Company, by bringing them cattle and other supplies from Ireland, he settled in the colony at a place called Newport's News. ‡ This gentleman is stated by several writers to have been the father of General Gookin; but the only circumstances authorizing even a conjecture to that effect, are the identity of name, and the fact that both lived in Virginia. A circumstance of an opposite character has been already alluded to, which seems to imply that Gookin had acquired his knowledge of arms in Kent; but, had he gone to Virginia with his father in 1621, when only about nine years of age, and re-

---

* Johnson's " *Wonderworking Providence,*" Chap. 26
† Purchas's *Pilgrims,* Vol. IV. p. 1785.
‡ Stith's *History of Virginia,* p. 205.

mained there until his removal to New England, as is supposed, he could not well have borne arms in Kent.

The Non-conformists were banished from Virginia in 1643; and in the following year, an "Indian Massacre" occurred in the same colony. "Upon these troubles," says Governor Winthrop, writing at that period, "divers godly disposed persons came from thence to New England." A ship containing a party of these exiles arrived at Boston, May 20th, 1644; and, as Gookin was admitted a freeman of the Colony on the 29th of the same month, he is supposed to have arrived in that ship.* He resided at first in Boston, and subsequently in Cambridge, where he was placed in command of the military force of the town. It seems probable from this circumstance that he brought with him some reputation for skill in the art of war, especially since he is described by a contemporary historian as "a very forward man to advance martial discipline." At a subsequent date, he was elected to the office of Major-General, or Commander-in-chief of the Colony; the governor at that period exercising no military command.

Soon after his settlement in Cambridge, Gookin was elected by the freemen of that town to represent them in the General Court, and, in 1651, he was chosen Speaker of the House of Deputies. The succeeding year, he became an assistant, or one of the general magistrates of the Colony. But the office to which he devoted the energies of the residue of a long life, was that of Superintendent of the Indians within the jurisdiction of Massachusetts. With the exception of two or three years passed in England, during the ascendency of Oliver Cromwell, he sustained this relation towards the Indians of the colony from the date of his first appointment in 1656, to his death, a period of more than thirty years. In conjunction with the excellent Eliot, he watched over their interests with the most unwearied care and anxiety, and sought every means to spread among them the blessings of civilization and Christianity.

The Commissioners of the United Colonies of New England, who were the agents of an English Corporation for Propagating the Gospel among the Indians, recommended, in one of their despatches to the government of the corporation, that a pecuniary allowance should be made to Gookin for his useful labors. "We have spoken," they write, "with Mr. Eliot and others, concerning Captain Gookin's employment among the Indians, in governing of them in several plantations, ordering their town affairs (which they are not able to do themselves), taking account of their labor and expense of their time, and how their children profit

---

* 2 Winthrop's *Hist. N. England*, p. 165. Note by Mr. Savage.

in their learning, with many things of a like nature, and find it is to be of much use and benefit to them, and therefore could not but desire him to go on in that work, and have ordered £15 to be paid him towards his expenses for the year past." This letter was dated at Boston, Sept. 18th, 1663. The recommendation was approved by the Corporation, who directed a similar sum to be paid to Mr. Gookin for another year. *

Unfortunately, however, the policy adopted by Gookin towards the Indians did not at all times escape the censure of the public ; for, during the troubles that arose from the aggressions of the hostile tribes, the people could with difficulty be restrained from involving in one common destruction the whole race ; and, while it required the most determined spirit on the part of the Superintendent to stem the torrent of popular violence, he did not fail to draw on himself undeserved odium and reproach. Gookin was eminently the friend of the Indians, and never hesitated to interpose his own safety between the infuriated white man, and the unoffending object of his vengeance. But the following pages will tell the story with the guileless simplicity of truth, and the sober dignity of conscious rectitude.

There is some satisfaction in knowing, that, during the latter part of his active career, Gookin enjoyed a full return of public favor and confidence. The same unshaken spirit of resistance to oppression, that had led him to protect the sons of the forest against popular injustice, again animated him when the agents of the Crown invaded the chartered rights of the Colony ; but in this contest his zealous efforts were rewarded by the smiles of general approbation.

He died at Cambridge, on the 19th of March, 1687, aged seventy-five years. A handsome monument was erected to his memory in the churchyard adjacent to the University, where he lies buried. He left three sons, one of whom was Sheriff of the County of Middlesex, and the others were reputable clergymen. One of his posterity, bearing the name of Daniel Gookin, was an officer in the American army during the Revolutionary war. There are now living, in various parts of the country, numerous lineal descendants of General Gookin, of the fifth and sixth generation.

Beside the present work, Gookin wrote a history of New England, which was never printed, and is now probably lost. The original manuscript, and only copy of it, is supposed to have been destroyed in the dwelling-house of his son, at Sherburne, Mass., which, with its contents, was consumed by fire. Another work, entitled " Historical

* 1 Hazard's *State Papers*, pp. 474 — 491.

Collections of the Indians in New England," &c., was first published by the Massachusetts Historical Society, in 1792.

For their MS. copy of the present work, the Antiquarian Society are indebted to Mr. JARED SPARKS, the learned editor of the WRITINGS OF WASHINGTON, and other valuable works, well known to the public. The following letter from Mr. Sparks to a member of the Council of the Society, contains all the information relating to the original MS. that has been obtained.

LETTER OF MR. SPARKS.

" *Cambridge, Sept. 4th,* 1835.

" DEAR SIR,

" The Rev. Dr. Harris has requested me to state to you what I know respecting the manuscript letter of Daniel Gookin to Robert Boyle, on the *Praying Indians,* which is about to be printed by the Antiquarian Society. I have very little knowledge of the matter. Five years ago, I obtained the manuscript from the Rev. Mr. Campbell, of Pittsburg, who had recently brought it from England. It was put into his hands by a clergyman in that country. Mr. Campbell loaned it to me. A copy was taken, and the original was returned to him. It bore every mark of antiquity, and I have no doubt of its genuineness. The manuscript was examined by Mr. Savage and Dr. Harris, who were also satisfied that the letter was written by Gookin. In short, the internal evidence is of itself a sufficient proof. Mr. Campbell told me that he had promised to return the original to its owner in England.

" I am, Sir, very respectfully,

" Your obedient servant,

" JARED SPARKS.

" JOSEPH WILLARD, Esq.,
    Boston."

The notes to the work have been chiefly supplied by Mr. Samuel G. Drake, of Boston, author of THE BOOK OF THE INDIANS, (of which the fifth edition has recently appeared,) to whom the Publishing Committee would here express their obligations.

The valuable documents immediately succeeding the History, it is believed, are now for the first time printed. The originals were furnished to the Committee by Mr. Lemuel Shattuck, of Boston, author of a *History of the Town of Concord.*

PUBLISHING COMMITTEE.

EPISTLE DEDICATORY.

For the Honorable ROBERT BOYLE, Esq., Governor
of the Right Honorable Corporation for Gospelizing
the Indians in New England.

Right Honorable: A few years since I presumed
to transmit to your honors a few historical collections
concerning the Indians in New England, especially
the Christian or Praying Indians, which script (as
things then stood) was a true account of that matter.
And were I to write it again (as things were then
circumstanced), I could not add or diminish from the
substance of it.* But since the war began between
the barbarous heathen and the English, the state of
affairs is much altered with respect to the poor Christian Indians, who are much weakened or diminished,
especially in the colony of Massachusetts in New
England. A true, impartial narrative whereof, and of
their doings and sufferings and present condition, I
have endeavoured to collect, and here humbly to offer

---

* Now contained in 1 Vol. 1st Ser. Coll. Mass. Hist. Soc.

for your Honors' perusal, who are, under God, as nursing fathers to this despised orphan : the reason of this my undertaking is intimated in the first page. All that is defective is the inability and unworthiness of the penman.   I humbly entreat your honors to pardon my boldness and weakness, and accept of the matter clothed in a wilderness dress, yet I trust agreeing with truth and verity.   The God of heaven and earth bless your Honors, and crown you all with spiritual, temporal, and eternal felicity, and make you more and more tender nursing fathers to Christ's interests and concerns among the English and Indians in New England; so prays

Your obliged servant
in this work of the
Lord Jesus Christ,

D. G.

Cambridge, in New England,
December 18th, 1677.

ELIOT'S LETTER.

The Reverend Mr. JOHN ELLIOT (teacher unto the Praying Indians) his Letter to the author of this Narrative upon his perusal of it.

Sir: I have perused this narrative of the Christian Indians, both their sufferings and doings; though (as you intimate) more might have been said, yet here is enough to give wise men a taste of what hath passed. Leave the rest unto the day of judgment, when all the contrivances and actings of men shall be opened before the seeing eye of a glorious Judge. I do not see that any man, or orders of men, can find just cause of excepting against (human frailties excepted) any thing that you have written. As natural fathers, so foster fathers, are well pleased to hear well of their children. I doubt not but the Right Honorable Corporation will well accept this great service and duty, to give them so clear an account of their foster children, a service which I confess I am not able to perform. The Lord bless your good and faithful labour in it. I do heartily and thankfully adjoin my attestation to the substance of all you have here written, and so rest

Your worships' to serve you,

JOHN ELLIOT.

HISTORY

OF THE

CHRISTIAN INDIANS.

A TRUE AND IMPARTIAL NARRATIVE OF THE DOINGS AND
SUFFERINGS OF THE CHRISTIAN OR PRAYING INDIANS,
IN NEW ENGLAND, IN THE TIME OF THE WAR BETWEEN
THE ENGLISH AND BARBAROUS HEATHEN, WHICH BE-
GAN THE 20th OF JUNE, 1675.

FORASMUCH as sundry persons have taken pains to write and
publish historical narratives of the war, between the English
and Indians in New England, but very little hath been hitherto
declared (that I have seen) concerning the Christian Indians,
who, in reality, may be judged to have no small share in the
effects and consequences of this war; I thought it might have
a tendency to God's glory, and to give satisfaction to such worthy and good persons as have been benefactors and well-willers
to that pious work of Gospelizing the poor Indians in New England, to give them right information how these Christian natives
have demeaned themselves in this hour of tribulation. And
therefore (through divine assistance) I shall endeavour to give
a particular and real account of this affair. Before I come to
declare matter of fact, I shall premise some things necessary to
be understood for the better clearing of our ensuing discourse.

The Christian Indians in New England have their dwellings
in sundry Jurisdictions of the English Colonies, and that at a
considerable distance from each other; more particularly,

1st. Upon the Islands of Nantucket and Martha's Vineyard,
in which two Islands there inhabit many hundreds of them that
visibly profess the Gospel.* These Indians have felt very little

---

* For interesting particulars respecting the Christian Indians on these

of this war comparatively ; for the English that dwell upon those Islands have held a good correspondency with those Indians all the time of the war, as they did before the war began.   The only sufferings of these Christian Indians was of their coming up in the summer, during the war, to work for the English in the Massachusetts Colony, whither many scores of them did usually repair to work, whereby they and their families were accommodated with necessary clothing, which is scarce and dear upon those Islands.   Besides, several of those Indians belonging to the Islands, being at work at some of the English towns when the war began in the summer, 1675, were not permitted to stay in the Colonies, but were forced to pack away to their own habitations to their great loss, because the English were so jealous, and filled with animosity against all Indians without exception.   Hereby they tasted but little of the effects of the war, and therefore they will not so properly fall under our consideration.

2dly. Another considerable number of Christian Indians live within the Jurisdiction of New Plymouth, called the Cape Indians ; these also (through God's favor) have enjoyed much peace and quiet by their English neighbours, and several of them have served the English in the war, especially in the heat of the war, and did acquit themselves courageously and faithfully.   Indeed, at the beginning of the war, the English of that colony were suspicious of them, and slow to improve any of them in the war, though divers of those Christian Indians manifested themselves ready and willing to engage with the English against their enemies: and this is so much the more remarkable that those Indians proved so faithful to the English interest, considering the war first began in the Colony of Plymouth, by the rashness and folly of Philip, Chief Sachem of the Indians in those parts, unto whom, or to some of his people doubtless, these praying Indians were allied by affinity or consanguinity.   Therefore good reason it is, to attribute it to the grace and favor of God, and to the efficacy of religion upon their hearts, that they carried it so well in this war ; the greatest sufferings these underwent was, being impeded by the war to come and work in harvest among the English, whereby they had a good helper to

Islands, see the Rev. Matthew Mayhew's *Brief Narrative, &c.* 12mo. Boston, 1694; and Experience Mayhew's *Indian Converts,* 8vo. London, 1727. In 1694, Mr. M. Mayhew reckoned there were " about three thousand " Christian Indians on Martha's Vineyard and the Islands adjacent.

get apparel. These also do not fall so properly under consideration in this narrative.

3dly. There were a few other praying Indians, about 40 persons, that began to embrace the Christian religion, who lived near to New Norwich, in Connecticut Colony, who were taught by that worthy and reverend minister, Mr. James Fitch, pastor at Norwich, who had taken much pains to declare the Gospel to the Indians in those parts. But the chief Sachem, Uncas, and his eldest son, Oineko,* not being encouragers of the Christian religion, (though otherwise they and their people have joined with the English in the war, and proved faithful, especially against their ancient and implacable enemies, the Narragansetts,) I say, this Sachem and people being generally averse to entertain Christian religion, or countenance any such as did among his people incline to it, hence it came to pass, that those few in those parts that prayed to God are not distinguishable from the rest, and so nothing of remark is spoken of any of them, and hence will not be subjects of this discourse.

4thly. The fourth and not the least company of Christian Indians, are those that inhabit the Jurisdiction or Colony of Massachusetts, who were taught and instructed in the Christian faith by that indefatigable servant of God and minister of Christ, Mr. John Eliot, (who hath also labored among all the praying Indians in New England, more or less, for about 30 years,) but more especially among those of Massachusetts Colony. And of these Indians, it is, I shall principally speak, who have felt more of the effects of this war than all the rest of the Christian Indians, as may appear in that which ensues.

For the better understanding of the following discourse, we are to know that all these praying Indians dwelt upon the south side of Merrimack river, and inhabited seven villages, viz. Wamesit,† Nashobah,‡ Okkokonimesit, alias Marlborough, Hassannamesit,§ Makunkokoag,|| Natick, and Punkapog,¶ alias Pakomit.

---

* Oneko, as commonly written.

† Formerly Chelmsford, now chiefly included in the city of Lowell.

‡ Near Nagog Pond in the present limits of Littleton. See Shattuck's *History of Concord.*

§ Grafton. In 1764, there were about 8 families remaining of the Hassanamesits.

|| Hopkinton.

¶ Stoughton. When not otherwise mentioned, these towns will be understood to be in the present limits of Massachusetts.

These were for distinction's sake called the *old* praying Indian
towns, for there were five or six small villages of the Nipmuck
Indians that had some people in them inclining to entertain the
Gospel, therefore were called, the *new* praying towns. But
those latter being but raw and lately initiated into the Christian
profession, most of them fell off from the English and joined
the enemy in the war, some few excepted, whose hearts God
had turned, that came in to Okkokonimesit, or Marlborough, and
lived among the praying Indians ; they were drawn together
there until such time as the one and other were driven and
drawn away among the enemy, as shall afterward (God willing)
be declared. I am therefore principally to speak of the Christian
Indians belonging to the old praying towns above mentioned.

The situation of those towns was such, that the Indians in
them might have been improved as a wall of defence about the
greatest part of the colony of Massachusetts; for the first named
of those villages bordered upon the Merrimack river, and the
rest in order about twelve or fourteen miles asunder, including
most of the frontiers. And had the suggestions and importunate
solicitations of some persons, who had knowledge and experience
of the fidelity and integrity of the praying Indians been attended
and practised in the beginning of the war, many and great mis-
chiefs might have been (according to reason) prevented ; for
most of the praying towns, in the beginning of the war, had put
themselves into a posture of defence, and had made forts for
their security against the common enemy ; and it was suggested
and proposed to the authority of the country, that some English
men, about one third part, might have been joined with those
Christian Indians in each fort, which the praying Indians
greatly desired, that thereby their fidelity might have been
better demonstrated, and that with the assistance and company
of some of those English soldiers, they might daily scout or
range the woods from town to town, in their several assigned
stations, and hereby might have been as a living wall to guard
the English frontiers, and consequently the greatest part of the
Jurisdiction, which, with the blessing of God, might have prevented the desolations and devastations that afterward ensued.
This was not only the suggestion of some English, but the
earnest desire of some of the most prudent of the Christian
Indians, who in all their actions declared that they were greatly
ambitious to give demonstration to the English of their fidelity
and good affection to them and the interest of the Christian re-

ligion, and to endeavour all that in them lay to abate and take off the animosity and displeasure that they perceived was enkindled in some English against them ; and hence it was that they were always found ready to comply cheerfully with all commands of the English authority. But such was the unhappiness of their affairs, or rather the displeasure of God in the case, that those counsels were rejected, and on the contrary a spirit of enmity and hatred conceived by many against those poor Christian Indians, as I apprehend without cause, so far as I could ever understand, which was, according to the operation of second causes, a very great occasion of many distressing calamities that befell both one and the other.

The great God who overruleth and ordereth all counsels and actions for the bringing to pass his own purpose and desire, was pleased to darken this counsel from such as had the power to put it in practice ; and although there was a demonstration, near hand, in the colony of Connecticut for the benefit of such a course as was before proposed and desired, in keeping a fair correspondence with their neighbour Indians, the Mohegans and Pequods, who were not only improved by the English in all their expeditions, but were a guard to the frontiers, whereby those Indians, upon the account of their own interest (for they had no principles of Christianity to fix them to the English), proved very faithful and serviceable to the English, and under God were instrumental for the preservation of that Colony which had but one small deserted village burnt in this war,* and very little of their other substance destroyed by the enemy. I have often considered this matter and come to this result, in my own thoughts, that the most holy and righteous God hath overruled all counsels and affairs in this, and other things relating to this war, for such wise, just, and holy ends as these ;

1st. To make a rod of the barbarous heathen to chastise and punish the English for their sins. The Lord had, as our faithful minister often declared, applied more gentle chastisements (gradually) to his New England people ; but those proving in great measure ineffectual to produce effectual humiliation and reformation, hence the righteous and holy Lord is necessitated to draw forth this smarting rod of the vile and brutish heathen,

---

* " All the buildings in Narraganset, from Providence to Stonington, a tract of about 50 miles, were burned, or otherwise destroyed."—Trumbull, *Hist. Con.* I. 351, *note.* The place destroyed was doubtless included in this tract, but its name is not given.

who indeed have been a very scourge unto New England, especially unto the Jurisdiction of Massachusetts.

2dly. To teach war to the young generation of New England, who had never been acquainted with it; and especially to teach old and young how little confidence is to be put in an arm of flesh; and to let them see if God give commission to a few (comparatively) of naked men to execute any work of God, how insignificant nothings are numbers of men well armed and provided, and endowed with courage and valor, to oppose and conquer the enemy, until God turn the balance. It was observed by some judicious, that, at the beginning of the war, the English soldiers made a nothing of the Indians, and many spake words to this effect, that one Englishman was sufficient to chase ten Indians;* many reckoned it was no other but *Veni, vidi, vici.* Surely the Lord well knew, that if he should have given his people victory, before they were in some measure corrected of this sin of trusting in arm of flesh, that little glory would accrue to his name by such a deliverance.

3dly. The purging and trying the faith and patience of the Godly English and Christian Indians, certainly was another end God aimed at in this chastisement. And the discovery of hypocrisy and wickedness in some that were ready to cry "Aha!" at the sore calamity upon the English people in this war, and as much as in them lay to overthrow God's work in Gospelizing the poor Indians.

4thly. Doubtless one great end God aimed at was the punishment and destruction of many of the wicked heathen, whose iniquities were now full; the last period whereof was their malignant opposition to the offers of the Gospel, for the Paka-

---

* This was no doubt true; and no remark on the contempt, in which the poor Indians were held by men on so many accounts to be venerated, can be more appropriate than the following note by Governor Hutchinson. "It seems strange," says he, "that men, who professed to believe, that God hath made of one blood all nations of men for to dwell on all the face of the earth, should so early and upon every occasion, take care to preserve this distinction. Perhaps nothing has more effectually defeated the endeavours for Christianizing the Indians. It seems to have done more: to have sunk their spirits, led them to intemperance, and extirpated the whole race." — *Col. Papers,* 151. This remark was made upon a passage in Major Gibbon's instructions, on being sent against the Narragansets in 1645, in these words: "You are to have due regard to the distance which is to be observed betwixt Christians and Barbarians, as well in wars as in other negotiations."

nahats * and the Narragansetts, those two great nations upon whom the dint of war hath most especially fallen, (for they are almost totally destroyed,) had once and again the Gospel offered to them. But their chief Sachems malignantly rejected and opposed it, and consequently the people followed their examples.† And notwithstanding they were very conversant among the English, especially the Narragansetts, and commendable for their industry and labor among the English, yet had the most of them no hearing ears unto the glad tidings of salvation offered in the Gospel, and very few of them delighted in communion with the Christian Indians. And here I shall insert a matter of remark. After the war began with Philip, the English, having cause to be suspicious of the Narragansetts, sent some soldiers to Mr. Smith's, of Wickford, that lived near them, designing thereby to put upon them a necessity to declare themselves friends or enemies, and to push upon them the performances of former articles of agreement between the English and them, at which time, being in July, 1675, they complied to a treaty‡ of continuing in peace and friendship with the English. But among other articles, the Narragansetts, by their agent Potuche,§ urged that the English should not send any among them to preach the Gospel or call upon them to pray to God. But, the English refusing to concede to such an article, it was withdrawn, and a peace concluded for that time. In this act they declared what their hearts were, viz. to reject Christ and his grace offered to them before. But the Lord Jesus, before the expiration of 18 months, destroyed the body of the Narragansett nation, that would not have him to reign over them, particularly all their chief Sachems and this Potuche, a chief Counsellor and subtle fellow, who was taken at Rhode Island, coming voluntarily there, and afterward sent to Boston and there executed.||

* Pokanokets, Philip's people.

† When Mr. Eliot tried to engage Philip's attention to religion, the Sachem, taking hold of a button on the good man's coat, said, he cared no more for his religion than for that button. — Mather's *Magnalia*. Mr. Mayhew requested of Ninigret, chief of the Narragansets, liberty to preach to his people; but the chief bid him go and make the English good first, and in effect added, that so long as the English could not agree among themselves what religion was, it ill became them to teach others. See Life of Ninigret in Drake's *Book of the Indians*.

‡ To be seen in Hubbard's *Narrative* and Hutchinson's *History*.

§ Potok.

|| Potok appears to have been a stern warrior chief. We can add but

5thly. And lastly, to mention no more, this doubtless was another end the God of Heaven aimed at in this war, that he might magnify his rich and free grace, in saving and delivering his poor New England people at last, and destroying the greater part of the enemy, and subduing others under them ; and this was by his own hand chiefly done, thereby magnifying his grace in answering the incessant prayers of the people of God in England, Ireland, and Scotland, as well as in New England. But I shall forbear to add any more of this kind, and proceed now to declare matter of fact.

In April, 1675 ,before the war broke forth above two months, there being, the March preceding, some agitations between the Government of Plymouth, and Philip, Sachem of Mount Hope, concerning the murder of one John Sasamand,* one of the Christian Indians belonging to Massachusetts ; but at that time he lived in Plymouth Colony, near Taunton,† and was a minister to some Christian Indians thereabouts. And Philip was vehemently suspected to be the contriver of this murder, though executed by others ; the story whereof is more particularly set down by Mr. Mather and Mr. Wm. Hubbard, in their histories of the war, which has spared me the labor to recite it in this place ; only thus much I may say, pertinent to my purpose, that this John Sasamand was the first Christian martyr of the Indians; for it is evident he suffered death upon the account of his Christian profession, and fidelity to the English. I say, about this time, the beginning of April, Waban,‡ the principal

---

little to the facts concerning him, in *The Book of the Indians.* It would seem, according to the author of "Letters to London," that he had been taken prisoner by the forces under Major Talcot ; for, after saying that they had killed the old Queen, Quaiapen, and Stone-wall John, the writer goes on, "Likewise *Potucke*, the great Indian counsellor, (a man, considering his education, of a wonderful subtlety,) was brought prisoner into Rhode Island." His residence was near Point Judith, in 1661. A complaint, signed by him and several others, to the government of Massachusetts, is on file in the State-House.

* Usually written Sassamon. In *The Book of the Indians* will be found a full account of this singular Indian ; as, besides the facts in Hubbard's and Mather's histories, the author has given from MS. records all the circumstances relating to the trial and execution of his alleged murderers.

† In Middleborough, near Assawomset Pond. The old chief Tuspequin, whose daughter he married, gave him lands to settle upon, and he preached for a time to his people.

‡ Written at first Wauban, whose name signified *a wind.* He was the first chief to profess Christianity, and entertained Mr. Eliot in his wigwam, at his first going among the Nipmucks as a preacher in their own language, 28 October, 1648.

Ruler of the praying Indians living at Natick, came to one of the magistrates on purpose, and informed him that he had ground to fear that Sachem Philip and other Indians, his confederates, intended some mischief shortly to the English and Christian Indians. Again, in May, about six weeks before the war began, he came again and renewed the same. Others also of the Christian Indians did speak the same thing, and that when the woods were grown thick with green trees then it **was** likely to appear, earnestly desiring that care might be had and means used for prevention, at least for preparation for such a thing; and a month after the war began. About the 21st of June, at the first going forth, the English were only employed as soldiers, excepting only three Indians for guides went with Capt. Prentice, viz. one James and Thomas Quannapohutt, alias Rumny Marsh,* and Zechary Abram, who all behaved themselves valiantly and faithfully. The English at first thought easily to chastise the insolent doings and murderous practices of the heathen. But it was found another manner of thing than was expected; for our men could see no enemy to shoot at, but yet felt their bullets out of the thick bushes where they lay in ambushments. The enemy also used this stratagem, to apparel themselves from the waist upwards with green boughs, that our Englishmen could not readily discern them, or distinguish them from the natural bushes; this manner of fighting our men had little experience of, and hence were under great disadvantages. The English wanted not courage or resolution, but could not discern or find an enemy to fight with, yet were galled by the enemy. The Council, having advice hereof from the commanders of the army, judged it very necessary to arm and send forth some of the praying Indians to assist our forces, hereby not only to try their fidelity, but to deal the better with the enemy in their own ways and methods, according to the Indian manner of fighting, wherein our Indians were well skilled, and had our [their] council practised,† and also to be as scouts and forlorns to the English; for the Indians generally excel in a quick and strong sight for the discovery of

---

* He was probably called Rumny Marsh from his having lived about that place, in Chelsea, near Boston. There has been a place of the same name in Kent, Eng., from time immemorial.

† The sense being incomplete here, some part of the sentence is probably wanting, or some word or words were mistaken by a transcriber. Probably, "*their* counsel." Compare page 445, line 8, and page 447, line 1.

any thing; and then they have a very accurate sagacity in discovering the tracks of man or beast.   And also they are subtle
and wily to accomplish their enterprise, especially they keep a
deep silence in their marches and motions, whereas the English
are more prone to talk to one another and make a noise,
whereby the enemy, discovering them before they come near,
either prepare for them or take their flight, as is most for their
advantage.   And here I shall take leave, as a parenthesis, to
insert a short and true story of an Indian chief, captain under
Uncas, who marching in this war as scout with some English
soldiers of Connecticut, one of the English soldiers had on a
new pair of shoes that made a creaking noise as they travelled.
The Indian captain was not quiet until he had persuaded the
fellow with creaking shoes to take his moccasins and wear
them, and the Indian carried the Englishman's shoes at his
back, and went himself barefoot.   Another English soldier had
on a pair of leather breeches, which being dry made a rustling
noise; the Indian captain was not satisfied until he had persuaded the man to take off his breeches, or else to wet them in
the water to prevent their rustling.   By this relation, which is
a truth, we may observe how circumspect and careful they are
in order to obtain advantage of their enemies.

1675, July 2. But to proceed to our purpose. The
Governor and Council gave their orders to Major Daniel
Gookin (unto whom a peculiar inspection and government of
the praying Indians was committed by authority of the General
Court) to raise a company of the praying Indians forthwith,
to be armed and furnished, and sent to the army at Mount
Hope.   In pursuance whereof the Major forthwith sent to all
the praying Indians for one third part of their able men, who
all readily and cheerfully appeared, and being enlisted were
about 52.*   These being armed and furnished were sent to
the army under conduct of Capt. Isaac Johnson,† the 6th of
July, 1675, who returned back after he had delivered them

---

* Hence the able men among the praying Indians at this time amount-
ed to about 156.   The old men, women, and children, were nearly 400,
as will be seen elsewhere stated.

† Capt. Johnson was one of the earliest emigrants to New England,
having been admitted a freeman of Massachusetts in 1635.   He resided
at Roxbury, and was elected Commander of the Ancient and Honorable
Artillery Company, (as the corps is now styled,) in 1667.   He was killed
at the taking of Narraganset fort, Dec. 19th, 1675.

to Major Savage, commander-in-chief of the army at Mount Hope. How those Indians behaved themselves I shall say little, not being an eye-witness thereof, but both Major Savage, Capt. Prentiss, and Capt. Henchman, chief officers in the army, give testimony that the most of them acquitted themselves courageously and faithfully, as may appear by a certificate (in the close of this treatise) under their hands.

At this time the praying Indians at Marlborough were increased to about 40 men, besides women and children; which came to pass by the advice of several Christian Indians that came to them, viz. from Hassanamesit, Magunkoag, Manchage,* and Chobonokonomum,† who (when the troubles increased) left their places, and came into Marlborough under the English wing, and there built a fort upon their own land, which stood near the centre of the English town, not far from the church or Meeting-House ; hence they hoped not only to be secured, but to be helpful to the English, and on this pass and frontier to curb the common enemy ; and in all probability it would have produced that effect, but the most holy God for the chastisement of the English and Indians disposed otherwise, as in the sequel will appear.

These Indians at Marlborough, some of them having been abroad to scout in the woods (according to the Englishmen's order) to discover the enemy and secure the place, they met with a track of Indians which they judged to be a greater number by the track, and upon discovery whereof they presently repaired to the chief militia officer of the town named Lieut. Ruddock, and informed him thereof, who presently joined some English with them, and sent forth to pursue the track, which they did, and first seized five Indians and after two more, which were in all seven ; these being seized were forthwith sent down to the magistrates at Cambridge, who examined them and found them to be Indians belonging to Narragansett, Long Island, and Pequod, who had all been at work about seven weeks with one Mr. Jonathan Tyng, of Dunstable, upon Merrimack river; and hearing of the wars they reckoned with their master, and getting their wages, conveyed themselves away without his privity, and being afraid marched secretly through the woods, designing to go to their own country, until they were intercept-

* Oxford.   † In Dudley.

ed as before.   This act of our Christian India
was an evident demonstration of their fidelit
interest.   The seven prisoners, after further c
the council, where they told the same thing a:
a few days committed to prison, but afterwards

But to return to our purpose.   Notwithstand
cate which hereafter follows, and is before touch
the courage and fidelity of our Christian Indi
Hope, yet I am not ignorant that some officers an
the army who had conceived much animosity against all indians,
disgusted our Christian Indian soldiers, and reported ultimately
concerning them, saying that they were cowards and skulked
behind trees in fight, and that they shot over the enemies'
heads, and such like reproaches; but, as the proverb says, Ill
will speaks no good; but certainly none could better know their
doings than their particular commanders, who have subscribed
the certificate, who are men not inferior to any in the army for
honesty and fidelity.   This I do also know upon my own personal knowledge, that some of those Indian soldiers at their
return (viz. John Hunter, Thomas Quannapohitt, and Felix)
brought to the governor, John Leverett, Esq., four of the enemies' scalps, slain by them at the fight at or near Mount Hope,
for which they had a reward given them.   In this expedition
one of our principal soldiers of the praying Indians was slain, a
valiant and stout man, named Job Nesutan; he was a very
good linguist in the English tongue, and was Mr. Eliot's assistant and interpreter in his translations of the Bible, and other
books of the Indian language.*   The loss of such a useful and
trusty man was great in the forementioned respects.   Besides,
another stout Indian of 86 was wounded by accident, and lost
the use of his right arm, his name Thomas Rumny Marsh,†
the manner thus; he, being a horseman, as is before hinted,
under Captain Prentiss, they being at a stand and he sitting on
his horse, set the butt end of a long gun he carried upon the
ground, and held his hand upon the muzzle of the gun which
was charged; the weather being hot, and the horse disturbed
by flies, pawed with his fore foot, and turning the cock, (which
was half bent,) the piece went off and tore his hand in pieces.

---

* Mr. Eliot "hired an old Indian, named Job Nesutan, to live in his
family, and teach him his language."   See *Book of the Indians*, ii. 111.
† Called oftener Quanapohit, the same already noticed.

It was after a long time cured, but the use of this hand lost; yet this fellow since that time hath done very good service as well as before, as may afterward be mentioned.

This company of praying Indians, part of them were sent home and disbanded after 25 days, and the other half were not disbanded until some time after Philip was fled out of his country, and those Indians were part of the number that pursued him; and had their counsel been practised, as I was credibly informed by some upon the place, he had probably been taken, and his distressed company at that time; but God darkened that counsel from us at that time, for Philip's iniquity being not yet full, and the Indian rod upon the English backs had not yet done God's errand.

About the 26th of July, fifty Mohegans belonging to Uncas, with three of his sons, whereof one was his eldest son and successor, named Oneko, came into Boston, all armed with guns, being conducted by two Englishmen and some of the praying Indians of Natick, where they lodged the night before; they brought a letter from Mr. James Fitch, minister of Norwich, to our Governor and Council, signifying that their Sachem Uncas had sent them to assist the English against their enemy Philip; these had given some intimations of the tender of their service some days before, by six messengers sent on purpose, but they were not expected to come so speedily as they did. July 29th, those 50 Mohegans and three of our praying Indians of Natick being joined with them for guides, were sent forth from Boston, conducted by Quarter-Master Swift, and a 'ply of horse, and were ordered at first (by the Governor of Plymouth, into which Colony they were to pass,) to march toward Taunton; but after they were upon their way, the Governor of Plymouth sent them other orders, to go to Rehobah, or Seekonk,* which he did unwittingly, not then knowing any thing of Philip's flight. But this thing was so ordered by the divine hand. For those Mohegans and Natick Indians came to Seekonk the night before that Philip and all his company, being judged about 500 of all sorts, men, women and children, passed on the end of Rehobah, within two or three miles of the town where the Mohegans and Naticks quartered. What forces could be speedily raised in those parts and got to quarter, to pursue Philip, which were not above ten from Taunton, thirty-four

* Formerly one town, now two. *Seekonk* or *Seakonk* is Indian.

from Providence, and thirty from Seekonk, all English, who
joining together with the Mohegans and Natick Indians made
about 128 men, these pursued the enemy vigorously upon the
first of August, being the Lord's Day, and came up with the
rear of the enemy about ten o'clock in the forenoon; the enemy had brought his best men into the war to oppose our forces
pursuers; but our men, and particularly the Mohegan and
Natick Indians, behaved themselves with such courage and
activity, as was certified by a letter from Mr. Newman, of
Rehobah, a minister that was present in the fight, that they
slew fourteen of the enemies, principally men, and wounded
divers others, whereof one Nimorod,* a chief Captain and
Councillor to Philip, was one slain; also they took a considerable booty which the Mohegan Indians loaded themselves with,
which, together with the extreme heat of the weather, and the
wounds of two or three of our side, (but none were slain of
eighty-six,) occasioned them to give over the chase for a time
to refresh themselves. In the interim, the enemy got such a
start before our men that they escaped, though Capt. Henchman, with about sixty-eight men, whereof above twenty were
of our Natick Indians, came up from Pokasit, where he kept
garrison, about noon that day, and pursued the enemy two or
three days, but could not come up with him, nor yet Capt.
Mosely, who was sent from Boston, with fifty dragoons, to
follow the chase, could not overtake the enemy, whose time
was not yet come. Our praying Indians with Capt. Henchman,
being not so loaded with plunder as the Mohegans, moved the
Capt. to send them to head the enemy. But he thought it
not prudent to break his small company, (for the Providence,
Taunton, and Seekonk men were all gone home,) and to hazard
so few as eight Indians were, against so considerable and numerous, as Philip was apprehended then to be. But as we
were also certainly informed that Philip was so distressed and
clogged at that time, his ammunition almost spent also, the
Squaw Sachem,† and her people, the Womponoges, (his
greatest strength,) drawn off from them to the Narragansetts,
that he had little above fifty able men left, but many hundreds
of old men, women, and children; so that if the counsel of our

* *Woonashum* was his Indian name.
† Namumpum, sister-in-law to Philip. She was now called Weeta-
moo, and her husband's name was Petananuit, or *Peter Nunuit*, as generally pronounced.

Christian Indians had been put in practice, according to rational probability they had taken or slain Philip, and so retarded his motion, that the rest might have come up with him and destroyed his party. But God's providence overruled those prudent suggestions, and permitted this, our arch enemy, to live longer, to be a scourge to us.

About the latter part of July, 1675, the Council sent Capt. Edward Hutchinson as a commissioner to treat with the Nipmuck Indians, and as a guard and assistant to him, Capt. Wheeler and twenty-five of his troops were sent with him, and three of our Christian Indians for guides and interpreters, named Joseph and Sampson, brothers, and sons to old Robin Petuhanit, deceased, a good man who lived at Hasanamoset, together with George Memecho, their kinsman: these three accompanied Captain Wheeler and Captain Hutchinson, and were with them at the swamp near Quabage, when the Nipmuck Indians perfidiously set upon our men and slew seven* of our men and wounded others; the Indian, George, was taken prisoner by the enemy, and came home afterward and brought good intelligence. The other two brothers, Joseph and Sampson, acquitted themselves very industriously and faithfully, and, by their care and skilful conduct, guided Captain Hutchinson and Captain Wheeler with their company in safety to Brookfield, an English town near adjacent, which was in a few hours after attacked by those Indians, and most of it burnt. They had only time to get together into one of the best houses, which was the same where the two wounded Captains Hutchinson and Wheeler were, with the remnant of their soldiers and the inhabitants, which, that night and the next day, was besieged and assaulted by the enemy, and divers attempts made to fire it. The particular relation of the matter is declared in the history of the wars,† and another

---

* Wheeler in his narrative says eight, and gives their names, as follows: Zachariah Philips of Boston, Timothy Farley of Bilerica, Edward Coleborn of Chelmsford, Samuel Smedly of Concord, Sydrach Hopgood of Sudbury, Sergeant Ayres, Sergeant Joseph Pritchard, and Corporal John Coy of Brookfield. Mr. Hubbard states the right number, but in the "Letter to London," [p. 20, Drake's edition,] sixteen are said to have been killed "at once."

† This valuable narrative, which appears to have been unknown to the historian Hutchinson, was reprinted in 1827, by the New Hampshire Historical Society, in the second volume of their Collections.

printed paper put forth by Capt. Wheeler, being a narrative
of the matter, wherein he mentions nothing of those Indians'
service, but yet gave them a certificate under his hand in
these words.

"These are to certify that Joseph and Sampson, Indians,
that were our guides in the Nipmuck country, behaved
themselves courageously and faithfully, and conducted our
distressed company in the best way from the swamp, where
we were wounded and divers slain, unto the town of Brookfield, and all the time of our being with them, in the inn
of Brookfield, when the enemy attacked us, those two Indians
behaved themselves as honest and stout men.

"Witness my hand, the 20th of August, 1675.

THOMAS WHEELER."

This certificate those Indians had, and I saw it, and took
a copy of it, and I spoke with Captain Wheeler before his
death,* and he owned it. Besides, James Richardson, now
Lieutenant, belonging to the army and living at Chelmsford,
and several others that were in that action and are yet alive,
owned the same thing; and moreover, both Captain Wheeler
and Lieutenant Richardson informed me that the two Indians
beforenamed, told Captain Hutchison, before the Indians perfidiously assaulted their company, that they much doubted the
fidelity of those Nipmuck Indians, and feared they would
be treacherous, and earnestly persuaded Capt. Hutchison and
the rest not to adventure to go to them at the swamp; and
gave him some demonstrations of it, for there were two English
there sent the day before the mischief, and they then observed
that which was a ground of their fears. But the Captain, being
a man of spirit and intent upon his trust, would proceed, and
so lost not only his own life but others also, for though he
was not killed upon the place, yet he died of his wounds
soon after.† But this shows the prudence and fidelity of the
Christian Indians; yet notwithstanding all this service they
were, with others of our Christian Indians, through the harsh

---

* He died 10th December, the next year, 1676. — *Farmer.*

† Namely, 19th August. From Brookfield he was carried to Marlborough, where he died. He was an ancestor of Governor Hutchinson,
the historian.

dealings of some English, in a manner constrained, for want of shelter, protection, and encouragement, to fall off to the enemy at Hassanamesit, the story whereof follows in its place; and one of them, viz. Sampson, was slain in fight, by some scouts of our praying Indians, about Watchuset; and the other, Joseph, taken prisoner in Plymouth Colony, and sold for a slave to some merchants at Boston, and sent to Jamaica, but upon the importunity of Mr. Elliot, which the master of the vessel related to him, was brought back again, but not released. His two children taken prisoners with him were redeemed by Mr. Elliot, and afterward his wife, their mother, taken captive, which woman was a sober Christian woman, and is employed to teach school among the Indians at Concord, and her children are with her, but her husband held as before, a servant; though several that know the said Joseph and his former carriage, have interceded for his release, but cannot obtain it; some informing authority that he had been active against the English when he was with the enemy. There were several others of our praying Indians employed for guides to the forces sent us by Major Willard,* to Brookfield, and with Capt. Lathrop and Lieut. Curtis and Daniel Champney, in several enterprises and affairs committed to them, both for the release of Brookfield, and to speak with the Nipmucks, before they broke out into hostility, all which Indians acquitted themselves faithfully according to their several employments and betrustments. But, notwithstanding those signal and faithful services done by those Christian Indians, and divers others not here related, yet the animosity and rage of the common people increased against them, that the very name of a praying Indian was spoken against, in so much, that some wise and principal men did advise some that were concerned with them, to forbear giving that epithet of praying.† This rage of the people, as I contend, was occasioned from hence. Because much mischief being done and English blood shed by the brutish enemy, and

* Major Simon Willard was an active officer during this war until his death, which took place 24th April, 1676, at Charlestown, where he was then holding a court.

† So obnoxious were the friends of the "Praying Indians" to the mass of the people, that Gookin said on the bench, while holding a Court, that he was afraid to go along the streets; and the author of "A Letter to London," says, "that his (Gookin's) taking the Indians' part so much, had made him a by-word among men and boys."

because some neighbour Indians to the English at Quabage, Hadley, and Springfield (though none of those were praying Indians) had proved perfidious and were become enemies, hence it was that all the Indians are reckoned to be false and perfidious. Things growing to this height among the English, the Governor and Council, against their own reason and inclination, were put upon a kind of necessity, for gratifying the people, to disband all the praying Indians, and to make and publish an order to confine them to five of their own villages, and not to stir above one mile from the centre of such place, upon peril of their lives. The copy of which order here follows.

"*At a Council held in Boston, August 30th, 1675.*

"The Council judging it of absolute necessity for security of the English and Indians in amity with us, that they be restrained their usual commerce with the English and hunting in the woods, during the time of hostility with those that are our enemies; do order, that all those Indians, that are desirous to approve themselves faithful to the English, be confined to the several places underwritten, until the Council shall take further order, and that they so order the setting of their wigwams that they may stand compact in one place of their plantations respectively, where it may be best for their own provision and defence, and that none of them do presume to travel above one mile from the centre of such of their dwellings unless in company of some English, or in their service, excepting for gathering in their corn with one Englishman in company, on peril of being taken as our enemies, or their abettors. And in case any of them be taken without the limits aforesaid except as above said, and do lose their lives, or be otherwise damnified by English or Indians; the Council do hereby declare that they shall account themselves wholly innocent, and their blood, or other damage by them sustained, will be upon their own heads. Also it shall not be lawful for any Indians, that are now in amity with us, to entertain any strange Indians, or to receive any of our enemies' plunder, but shall from time to time make discovery thereof to some English that shall be appointed for that end to sojourn with them, on penalty of being accounted our enemies, and to be proceeded against, as such.

"Also, whereas it is the manner of the heathen that are now in hostility with us, contrary to the practice of civil nations, to execute their bloody insolences by stealth, and skulking in small parties, declining all open decision of the controversy, either by treaty or by the sword; the Council do therefore order, that after the publication of the provision aforesaid, it shall be lawful for any person, whether English or Indian, that shall find any Indian travelling in any of our towns or woods, contrary to the limits abovenamed, to command them under their guard and examination, or to kill and destroy them as they best may or can. The Council hereby declaring, that it will be most acceptable to them, that none be killed or wounded, that are willing to surrender themselves into custody.

"The places of the Indians' residence are, Natick, Punquapog, Nashobah, Wamesit, and Hassanamesit. And if there be any that belong to other places, they are to repair to some one of these.

"By the Council.

EDWARD RAWSON, *Secretary.*"

By this order (which the Council was in a manner necessitated to put forth to quiet the people) the poor Christian Indians were reduced to great sufferings, being hindered from their hunting and looking after their cattle, swine, and getting in their corn, or laboring among the English to get clothes, and many other ways incommoded; also, were daily exposed to be slain or imprisoned, if at any time they were found without their limits. And there wanted not some English (ill willing to them), that took occasion to seize upon them, and take away their guns, and detain them to this day, and to bring them to prison. And whereas it was ordered and intended by the Council, that two or three Englishmen should be kept at every one of the Indian plantations aforesaid, to inspect their carriage and conversation, (which thing the Indians earnestly desired,) but few were found willing to live among them, only at Natick two persons were persuaded to reside, viz. John Watson, senior, and Henry Prentiss, of Cambridge; and for a short space some others took turns to keep at Punkapog, but they were changed weekly, and so I have not an account of their names. But those two above-named sojourned with the Natick Indians (where were the greatest number) for many weeks, yea, until they were removed to Deer Island. And those two persons were men of good credit for piety and honesty, who did give a very good testimony of the honest and sober deportment of those Indians, which appears by the certificate following, subscribed by them.

"Whereas we, John Watson, senior, and Henry Prentiss, were appointed by the Hon'ble Council of Massachusetts, in New-England, to reside among the praying Indians living at Natick, to observe and inspect their manners and conversation, which service we attended for about twelve weeks: during all this time, we carefully observed their carriage and demeanor, and do testify on their behalf, that they behaved themselves both religiously towards God, and respectively, obediently, and faithfully to the English; and in testimony of the truth hereof, we have hereunto set our hands, the   of   1677.

JOHN WATSON, Senior,
HENRY PRENTISS."

I have also spoken with some of the English that inspected the Indians at Punkapog, and in particular with Quartermaster Thomas Swift, who testified the same thing for substance, concerning the Christian Indians living there; and he also said that others who were there affirmed the same thing. By all these testimonies (and many others that might be produced if need required) it is most evident, that the jealousies and suspicions of some Englishmen concerning those poor Christians were groundless and causeless, which will more evidently appear hereafter; and one thing I shall here add, that Corporal John Watson before named (a discreet and sober man) hath more than once spoken in my hearing, that, before he sojourned among these Christian Indians, he had entertained much animosity, prejudice, and displeasure in his mind, against them, and judged them such as they were vulgarly represented to be. But after he had some time lived with them, he received such full satisfaction, and was so fully convinced of his former error, that he said he was ashamed of himself for his harsh aspersion of them only upon common fame; and this he testified, not only in my hearing, but before the Governor and Council, and General Court, and many others that inquired of him how the Indians carried it. So that he became an apologist for them, as occasion was offered, insomuch that some accounted him also an offender for so speaking.

Notwithstanding the Council's endeavours in the former

orders, and the testimony of these English witnesses on behalf of the Christian Indians, yet the clamors and animosity among the common people increased daily, not only against those Indians, but also all such English as were judged to be charitable to them. And particularly, many harsh reflections and speeches were uttered against Major Daniel Gookin, and Mr. John Elliot, the former of whom had been appointed by the authority of the General Court of Massachusetts, and approbation of the Honorable Governor and Corporation for Gospelizing those Indians, to rule and govern those Indians about twenty years, and the latter had been their teacher and minister about thirty years, as if they did support and protect those Indians against the English; whereas (God knows) there was no ground for such an imputation, but was a device and contrivance of Satan and his instruments, to hinder and subvert the work of religion among the Indians; for neither had any of our Christian Indians been justly charged, either with unfaithfulness, or treachery towards the English, since the war begun (that I know of.) But on the contrary, some of them had discovered the treachery, particularly Walcut the ruler of Philip, before he began any act of hostility, as is before mentioned, and since the war have served the English faithfully, but yet must be content to receive such retribution from too many, (at whose hands they have deserved other things,) but now both the Christian Indians, and all that favored them are enemies to the English, and ought to be proceeded against accordingly, if some men might have had their wills, so great was the rage and unreasonable prejudice of many at this time. It might rationally have been considered, that those two persons above-named, who had (one of them for above twenty years, and the other about thirty years,) been acquainted with, and conversant among those Christian Indians, should have more knowledge and experience of them than others had, and consequently should be able to speak more particularly concerning such of those Indians whom they knew (according to a judgment of charity) to be honest and pious persons. And if at such a time, they should have been wholly silent and remiss in giving a modest testimony concerning them when called thereunto, God might justly have charged it upon them, as a sin and neglect of their duty, had they for fear declined to witness the truth for Christ, and for these his poor distressed servants, some of the Christian Indians. And in this day of

Massah and Meribah, some that have the repute and I hope truly godly men, were so far gone with the temptation, that they accounted it a crime in any man to say that they hoped some of those Indians were pious persons, or that they had grounds of persuasion that such and such would be saved. This cruel frame of spirit (for I can give it no gentler denomination) arose I apprehend from a double ground, first, the malice of Satan against Christ's work among those Indians and to hinder their progress in religion; for they finding Englishmen, professing Christian religion, so enraged against them, and injurious to them without cause, as they well knew in their own consciences, whatever others thought or spake to the contrary, this was a sore temptation to such weak ones and little children as it were in the ways of Christianity, and hereby to incline them to apostasy, and if the devil by this stratagem could have prevailed, then the whole work of Christ among them, so spoken of, blessed and owned by the Lord, would have been utterly overthrown; this would have gratified Satan and his instruments greatly.

A second root of this trouble arose from the perfidious and unfaithful dealing of the wicked Indians, and their causeless rage and cruelty and fury against the English, and particularly the Springfield and Northampton Indians, who lived near the English and seemed to carry it fair for a time, but at last proved perfidious and treacherous. But there was not one of them that ever I heard of, that was a pretender to Christian religion. This defection of those Indians (though some near the mark have been ready to say that if they were prudently managed as others of their neighbours the Mohegans were, they might have continued in amity and been helpful to the English to this day,) but their defection at this time had a tendency to exasperate the English against all Indians, that they would admit no distinction between one Indian and an-other, forgetting that the Scriptures do record that sundry of the heathen in Israel's time, being proselyted to the Church, proved very faithful and worthy men and women; as Uriah the Hittite, Zeleg the Ammonite, Ithmah the Moabite, 1st Chron. xi. 39, 41, 46. And Rahab the harlot, and Ruth the Moabitess, and divers others, men and women. But this is no wonder that wicked men, yea, sometimes godly men, are angry and displeased with others that fear God, and too readily pass judgment on them that they are hypocrites and

naught, especially if there be occasion given by the falls of
any that profess religion. And because this is a matter of
moment I shall now come in order to relate a true story of the
sufferings of several of the Christian Indians about this time,
which, with the circumstances about it, and consequences of
it, proved matter of great offence to the English and Indians,
and laid a foundation of very much trouble and affliction not
only to the Indians but the English also, and a cause why
some of them afterwards were put upon the temptations to
be willing to go away with the enemy. Being surprised by
the enemy at a remote place, where they were gathering their
corn, and they being generally unarmed could not defend
themselves, and so were necessitated to comply with the
enemy. But of the particular account of the matter I shall
have occasion to speak hereafter if God please, and therefore
shall pass it now. On the 30th of August, one of the captains *
of the army (being instigated thereunto by some people of
those parts, no lovers of the Christian Indians,) sent down to
Boston with a guard of soldiers, pinioned and fastened with
lines from neck to neck, fifteen of those Indians that lived
with others of them upon their own lands, and in their own
fort at Okonhomesitt near Marlborough, where they were
orderly settled and were under the English conduct, and
frequently improved to scout about the plantation, and that
to the very great satisfaction and acceptance of many wise and
prudent men of the place; and besides they were ready to be
for guides and pilots to our soldiers that passed that way to
the westward, and had been often improved upon that account;
which things were done before. And though afterward these
Indians, by the procurement of some of their back friends, were
to be removed from this place to one of the other five allowed
places, which order before mentioned was made but the same
day they were seized, viz. the 30th of August, 1675, and
so it took not yet place, and these Indians were orderly settled
here at this time; and it had been well for the country and
for Marlborough in particular if they had never been disobliged
or removed from thence; I conceive it might have been instrumental to save many a man's life and much loss otherwise;
for this company of Indians in this place, had they been
cherished, conducted, and assisted by the English, would accord-

---

* Captain Samuel Mosely. — *Letter to London.*

ing to an eye of reason been as a wall of defence to the western frontiers of Massachusetts Colony ; where most of our danger lay, and where most mischief was afterwards done. But the counsel of the Lord must stand, and his purpose to chastise the poor English very sharp, and Indians also, must be accomplished ; therefore good counsel was hid from us, and jealousies and animosities increased and fomented among us. I shall not here recite the reasons moving the instigators unto this action, though I have seen and could produce the copy of the petition of Senonatt unto the Council, about this time. But there are some ready to conjecture that the occult and main reason inducing some of them to desire to be rid of the neighbourhood of those Indians, was in respect of a fair tract of land, belonging to them (near Marlborough) not only by natural right but by a grant from the General Court in the Massachusetts Colony ; and this is more latent now than heretofore, for some of the people of those parts have very lately, in the spring 1677, not only taken away the fencing stuff from about the Indians' lands, but taken away some cart-loads of their young apple trees and planted them in their own lands. And when some of those Indians made some attempts to plant (by order from authority) upon their own lands in the spring 1677, some person of that place expressly forbid them, and threatened them if they came there to oppose them, so that the poor Indians being put into fears returned, and dared not proceed ; and yet those Indians that went to plant were such as had been with the English all the war, and were not at all obnoxious. But I have been longer than I intended in the preface to that matter, fain to relate ; the pretence for seizing these fifteen Marlborough Indians and sending them down as prisoners was this, that eleven of them had committed a notorious murder upon seven English persons at Lancaster upon a Lord's day, August 22d ; the next and immediate accuser of these Indians was one David, an Indian, one of the fifteen, who being suspected for shooting at a lad belonging to the English of Marlborough that was sent out by his master to look up some sheep, this David being apprehended by the aforesaid captain upon the former suspicion, and fastened to a tree to be shot to death, and fearing to drink of the same cup as his brother Andrew had done a fortnight before, being shot to death by some soldiers at the same place.* Indeed An-

---

* About 21st August, 1675, "Capt. Mosely took two Indians, the

drew, having been several months before the war gone upon a hunting voyage towards the Lakes and French plantations, returning home a month before this time, fell into the enemies' quarters about Quabage, and was charged to be present with the Indians at the swamp when they did that perfidious villany against Captain Wheeler and Captain Hutchinson, before touched; but, some time after, he and his son-in-law left the enemy and came into the woods near Marlborough, where they were taken by Indian scouts belonging to Marlborough, and particularly by some of them now accused; and Andrew, brought to the English, was accused of being with the enemy at Quabage, and so immediately shot to death without acquainting the Council before it was done; for which the actors incurred blame, because there might have been good use made of his examination before his death, to have understood the state and numbers of the enemy; indeed, had it not been a boisterous season at this time, the actors would have been more severely animadverted upon. But David, as aforesaid, being fastened to a tree, and guns bent at him, feared death, and being offered a reprieve if he would confess truth, he promised something, and so was unbound, and then accused eleven of the Indians then at the fort, and now prisoners, to be murderers of the English at Lancaster before mentioned; "but," said he, "I did not see it done, neither was I there, but I heard some speak so." David was hereupon released from present death, but yet was sent down prisoner with the rest, and being examined before the Council, he at first owned that he had said so to the Captain, at Marlborough; but afterward, upon the trial

---

father and his son, and willing to examine them both apart, proceeded thus: Took the old man and bound him to a tree; after he was so bound, he sent away the son by a file of men out of sight; the old man there confessed he was a praying Indian, and that he was only hunting for deer thereabouts, but said his son was one of those men that wounded Capt. Hutchinson. So then, after they had pumped him as hard as they could, they fired a gun with no bullet in it over his head, untied him, and sent him another way with a file out of sight; then brought they his son, bound in like manner; they telling him that they had shot his father, and would shoot him also, if he would not confess what he was and what he knew. He fairly told them he was a praying Indian, but his father made him go with him to the Nipmoog Indians, and that there they shot three or four times apiece; whereupon they then brought the old man and tied him to his son, and examined them together; at length they confessed they were both among the Nipmoogs, and that the son did wound Capt. Hutchinson. After their examination they were both shot to death." — *Letter to London*, Drake's Ed.

before the court and jury, he said he had accused those Indians falsely. Indeed some of the accused Indians, particularly one named James Akompanet, a very understanding fellow, pleaded in behalf of himself and the rest, that what David said against them, was, 1st, to save his own life when he was bound to the tree, 2dly, to revenge himself of them because they had seized upon his brother Andrew, and his son, and delivered them to the English, one whereof was put to death, and the other sent out of the country, a slave.*
There were several things alleged against the prisoners. The most material were, that they were tracked from Lancaster to Marlborough about the time the murder was committed. That one of them had a pair of bandoleers belonging to one of the persons slain. That another had on a bloody shirt. But when the poor Indians had answered for themselves, and by good evidence cleared matters, all those pleas were figments : for the Indians proved by many witnesses, that they were all at Marlborough the whole Sabbath day, at the worship of God in their fort, and at the very time the murder was committed at Lancaster, ten miles distant ; that the bandoleers, that one of them had, he came honestly by ; and that they were delivered at Mount Hope, by one of the commissioners, unto James Rumny Marsh, an Indian soldier there, and delivered to him to bring home for him. The commissioner, Mr. Morse, owned in court that he had delivered a pair of bandoleers to James, and he, being in court, witnessed that he sent them home by the Indian accused. That the shirt became bloody by venison newly killed by those Indians, whereof this man carried a part upon his back; for it was made evident that those eleven Indians, with others, were abroad hunting, the Saturday before, towards Lancaster, and had killed three deer which they divided among them, (as their manner is,) and returned to their fort in Marlborough same Saturday evening. And others of them had bloody shirts upon the same occasion, besides the person accused. So that upon the trial were acquitted, except one man, who was found guilty of being accessary to the murder ;· but this man, named Joseph Spoonant, was tried by another jury, not the same that tried the others. Upon what ground the jury went, I know not ; but the man was sold for a slave, and sent out of the coun-

---

* They were both shot, as would seem by the authority cited in the last note.

try. Also, the first adviser of them all, called David, was condemned to be sold, his crime alleged for suspicion of shooting an Irish boy at Marlborough, and for accusing the others falsely; but all the rest were discharged. Before the conclusion of the trial, God in his providence so ordered, that two prisoners of the enemy were taken at two distinct times, who both declared that the murder at Lancaster (for which those men were accused) was committed by some of Philip's party, and particularly the conductor of the party, (which consisted of about twenty Indians,) was named John with one eye,* a notable fellow, that did very much mischief to the English afterward ; and this man did live near Lancaster before the war began, and was well acquainted with the place, and was a principal captain that conducted the Indians that burnt the town of Lancaster afterward ; and the prisoners before mentioned heard this one-eyed John boast of this exploit in slaying the people at Lancaster, for which our praying Indians were accused. But before this business was fully examined and issued, the clamors of the people were very great upon this occasion, and all things against those praying Indians accused (as one of the most intelligent of the magistrates said) were represented as very great, as things appear in mist or fog. Some men were so violent that they would have had these Indians put to death by martial law, and not tried by a jury, though they were subjects under the English protection, and not in hostility with us ; others had received such impressions in their minds, that they could hardly extend charity to the jurors and magistrates that acquitted them. And indeed God hath since, by his immediate hand, given testimony against some persons that were violent in it, to have them put to death, as I could instance in particulars,† but shall endeavour to avoid all personal reflections ; but

---

* His Indian name was Monoco. — See *Book of the Indians.*

† "But so it was," says the author of the *Letter* to which we have so often referred, "that, by one and two at a time, most of these eight Indians (and four more sent afterwards on the same account) were let loose by night, which so exasperated the commonalty, that about the 10 Sept., at nine o'clock at night, there gathered together about forty men, (some of note,) and came to the house of Capt. James Oliver. Two or three of them went into his entry to desire to speak with him, which was to desire him to be their leader, and they should join together and go break open the prison, and take one Indian out thence and hang him. Capt. Oliver, hearing their request, took his cane and cudgelled them stoutly, and so for that time dismissed the company."

(*recondam in corde meo*) I will lay up these things in my heart. Although I mention the story of this matter in this place, yet it was towards the latter end of September, before these Indians were tried and acquitted, all which time they remained in prison, under great sufferings. In truth, as the proverb is, every stone was turned by their enemies to bring them to destruction. But some, that were more considerate, serious, and pious, had their hearts exercised with tremblings in prayer all this time, lest the wind of temptations might blow so hard as to drive the judges and jurors upon the rock of bringing blood upon the land, which, blessed be God, was prevented in this matter.* But, as a further aggravation of the pretended faults of those Christian Indians at Marlborough, (which at this time lived there in a fort. and were a bulwark to the English inhabitants, and daily scouts ranged the woods adjacent to guard the English as well as themselves.) But God hid this benefit from the English, which should have been answered and requited with love and thankfulness; but, instead thereof, many of the English at that place were jealous of the Indians, their neighbours, and hated them, and took counsel to disoblige them. For the day before the Captain came to seize the prisoners above mentioned, the Lieutenant of the town, named Ruddock, demanded the delivery of their arms and ammunition, which they readily submitted to, and carried to his house twenty-three guns, and their powder-horns and bullets, that they used to carry with them, all which they laid at his feet. But their common stock of powder and ball, which was about ten pounds of powder, and sixty pounds of bullets, that was given to them by order of the commissioners of the United

* But by the authority last cited it seems blood was shed, and yet it is difficult to conceive that Mr. Gookin should omit to notice it. After relating what has been given in the preceding note concerning the mob and Capt. Oliver, that author says, "However, an order was issued out for the execution of that one (notorious above the rest) Indian, and accordingly he was led by a rope about his neck to the gallows. When he came there, the executioners (for there were many) flung one end over the post, and so hoisted him up like a dog, three or four times, he being yet half alive and half dead. Then came an Indian, a friend of his, and with his knife made a hole in his breast to his heart, and sucked out his heart's blood; being asked his reason therefor, his answer, '*Umh, Umh nu;* me stronger as I was before. Me be so strong as me and he too. He be ver strong man man fore he die.' Thus with one dog-like death (good enough) of one poor heathen, was the people's rage laid in some measure."

Colonies, paid for by the Indian stock in the disposal of the honorable Corporation at London; which common stock Lieutenant Ruddock very well knew of, for the principal Indians who kept the same had made him privy to it, when they first fetched it from Boston in the beginning of the war, as all the other praying Indians had their proportion, for their defence against the common enemy. But all this notwithstanding, it was alleged and pleaded in the court at the trial of the eleven Indians, as an artifice to render them all perfidious and treacherous to the English, that they had concealed a great quantity of powder and ball, and hid it in the ground in the fort, yet pretended to deliver all to the Lieutenant; for the Captain and soldiers, when they seized the prisoners, or not long after, ransacked the fort, and finding this common stock of ammunition, and three or four guns more (which some men, that were abroad when the former were delivered, had brought into the fort) afterward were seized. This matter was much talked of, and great clamors made against those poor Christians about it. But when the chiefest of the praying Indians of Marlborough had liberty to make answer for themselves, things were so fully cleared, that neither dishonesty, perfidiousness, or lying could be imputed to them touching those things. But yet notwithstanding, all their arms and ammunition, surrendered and seized (which to them was a very considerable matter) at such a time, and was their own property, yet was taken away and squandered by the soldiers and others, and never restored to the Indians to this day that I know of, nor any satisfaction for them, though some time afterward the Council ordered some persons to take account of those arms and ammunition, but nothing could be gotten. And though at the trial it was multiplied to a great quantity, now it was alleged that it was a small matter, and the soldiers had shared it as plunder among them, and nothing could be recovered.

But now I have done with the story of those poor Christian Indians at Marlborough; for it was not long after, they were all forced to retire from thence. I am sorry I have been so long upon this story, which I had not done, but it was a foundation and beginning of much trouble, that befell both the English and Indians afterwards.

I had need apologize for this long story concerning the Indians. But the true reason of being so particular is, that I might, in the words of truth and soberness, clear the innocency

of those Indians unto all pious and impartial men, that shall
peruse this script; and so far as in me lies, to vindicate the hand
of God and religion, that these Christians profess and practise;
and to declare I cannot join with the multitude, that would cast
them all into the same lump with the profane and brutish
heathen, who are as great enemies to our Christian Indians as
they are to the English.   For though some of them were captivated by the enemy, and escaped with their lives, (so, many
of the English that were taken captive also did,) yet this I
observed all along in this war, that the wicked Indians (our
enemies) did very industriously endeavour to bring the Christian
Indians into disaffection with the English, and to this end raised
several false reports concerning them, as if they held a correspondency with them, and on the other side sent their secret
messages to the Christian Indians that the English designed,
in the conclusion, to destroy them all, or send them out of the
country for bond slaves; and indeed, if the conscientious and
pious rulers of the country had not acted contrary to the
minds of sundry men, this last might have proved too true.

    1675, Sept. 7th.   The Council gave orders to Lieutenant
Thomas Henchman, of Chelmsford, to send out an Indian
messenger or two,* with a safe conduct, to Wannalanset,
Sachem of Naamhok,† who with some few others (related to
him) had withdrawn into the woods for fear, and quartered
about Penagoog; ‡ this Sachem being a wise man, and true to
the English, and a great lover of our nation, presuming the

---

* With these messengers was sent the following letter: "This our
writing or safe conduct doth declare, that the governor and council of
Massachusetts do give you and every of you, provided you exceed not
six persons, free liberty of coming unto and returning in safety from the
house of Lieut. T. Henchman, at Naamkeake, and there to treat with
Capt. Daniel Gookin, and Mr. John Eliot, whom you know, and [whom]
we will fully empower to treat and conclude with you upon such meet
terms and articles of friendship, amity, and subjection, as were formerly
made and concluded between the English and old Passaconaway, your
father, and his sons and people; and for this end we have sent these messengers [   ] to convey these unto you, and to bring your answer,
whom we desire you to treat kindly, and speedily to despatch them back
to us with your answer.   Dated in Boston, 1 Oct. 1675.   Signed by order of the Council.   *John Leverett,* Gov'r.
                                               Edw. Rawson, Sec'r."

† The same as Naamkeake, since called Amoskeag, now in Hookset,
New Hampshire.

‡ Pennakook, since Concord, N. H.

English were highly provoked against all Indians, he thought it best prudence to withdraw far into the country until the wars were abated, and accordingly did so, about six weeks before. The messengers sent could not meet him, but they sent their message to him; but he could not be prevailed with to return, but travelled up into the woods further afterward, and kept about the head of Connecticut river all winter, where was a place of good hunting for moose, deer, bear, and other such wild beasts; and came not near either to the English, or his own countrymen, our enemies. And now I am speaking of this Sachem, Wannalanset, I shall mention a few things concerning him, that are of remark, declaring his honesty, love, and fidelity to the English. This man is the eldest son living of the ancient and great Sachem living upon Merrimack river, called Passaconaway; who lived to a very great age, for I saw him alive at Pawtucket, when he was about 120 years old. This old Sachem, who was reputed a powow, or wizzard, was accounted a wise man; and possibly might have such a kind of spirit upon him as was upon Balaam, who in xxiii. Numbers 23, said, " Surely there is no enchantment against Jacob, neither is there any divination against Israel ;" and so this man in effect said concerning the English in New England; therefore this old Sachem thought it his best prudence for himself and posterity to make a firm peace with the English in his time, and submitted to them his lands and people, as the records of Massachusetts in New England declare; which peace and good correspondency he held and maintained all his life, and gave express commands to his sons, especially to this Wannalanset, that he should inviolably keep and maintain amity and friendship with the English, and never engage with any other Indians in a war against them.* This Sachem, his successor, was very careful always to observe and keep his father's engagements and commands, and hath often spoken of it to the English, declaring his purpose and resolution to continue so. The old Sachem, as I noted before, was reputed a very wise and know-

---

* "One much conversant with the Indians," says Mr. Hubbard, " about Merrimack river, being Anno 1660, invited by some Sagamores or Sachems to a great dance, Passaconaway, the great Sachem of that part of the country, intending at that time to make his last and farewell speech to his children and people, that were then all gathered together, to whom he addressed himself," &c. The speech is, in substance, as related in the text.

ing man, and a powow.   He would sometimes speak his appre-
hensions to his sons and people of the growing greatness of the
English in his land, and that if at any time the Indians did war
with them, it would but be in order to the destruction of the
Indians.   This present Sachem follows his father's steps in his
love and fidelity to the English; but moreover, through the
grace of Christ about four or five years since, he did embrace the
Christian religion, after some time of very serious consideration
and hearing God's word preached; * and I have charity and
faith to believe him to be an honest Christian man, being one
that in his conversation walks answerably to his knowledge.
He prays in his family, and is careful of keeping the Sabbath,
loves to hear God's word, sober in conversation.   After he
was withdrawn for fear, as is before touched, there was a
company of English soldiers, about one hundred, sent under
Capt. Mosely, to Pennagog, where it was reported there
was a body of Indians; but it was a mistake, for there was
above one hundred in all of the Pennagog and Namkig
Indians, whereof Wannalanset was chief.   When the English
drew nigh, whereof he had intelligence by scouts, they left
their fort and withdrew into the woods and swamps, where they
had advantage and opportunity enough in ambushment, to
have slain many of the English soldiers, without any great
hazard to themselves; and several of the young Indians inclined
to it, but the Sachem Wannalanset, by his authority and
wisdom, restrained his men, and suffered not an Indian to
appear or shoot a gun.   They were very near the English,
and yet though they were provoked by the English, who
burnt their wigwams and destroyed some dried fish, yet not
one gun was shot at any Englishman.   This act speaks much
for him, which himself and some of his men have related to
some of his English friends since his return.   Besides, he had
messengers sent to him more than once from the enemy,

* Wannalanset was about fifty-five years of age in 1674; always
friendly to the English, but unwilling to be importuned about adopting
their religion.   When he had got to be very old, however, he submitted to their desires in that respect.   When he had brought his
mind to believe in Christianity, he is reported to have said, "I must
acknowledge 1 have all my days been used to pass in an old canoe,
and now you exhort me to change and leave my old canoe, and em-
bark in a new one, to which I have hitherto been unwilling; but now
I yield up myself to your advice, and enter into a new canoe, and
do engage to pray to God hereafter."

soliciting him to join with them, but he always refused; and after he understood by messengers sent to him by Major Richard Waldron,* that he might come in to the English with safety, he complied with it, and came in with his relations to Cochecho, where Major Waldron lived, and was instrumental to bring in others; and now he *is* returned again under the English protection to his own place near Chelmsford, though but there a few people with him of his near friends, the rest being dead and fled from him either among their friends or enemies, and now he lives quietly and peaceably as heretofore, upon his own land.†

About this time ‡ the Pankapog § Indians brought into Boston and before the Council some prisoners of the enemy, that they had taken in the woods, particularly a noted Indian that lived near Taunton, called Drummer; and two more also they brought in, one of their own company named Caleb, whom they had accused for complotting to run away to Narragansett with another man's wife, and a young man that he had enticed to go with him, all which persons were secured. These actions of the praying Indians of Penkapog, as well as many others, are demonstrations of their fidelity to the English.

September 9th, 1675, there came to Boston Oneko, eldest son to Unkas, Sachem of Mohegan, with about twenty-eight Indians with him; their business was with the Commissioners of the United Colonies, then sitting in Boston; their petition consisted of three heads. 1st. They complained that a party of the Narragansets had by force taken from a small company of theirs about one hundred prisoners of Philip's people. 2dly. They desired the confirmation and assurance of their ancient inheritance of land at Mohegan and Wabaquisit.‖ 3dly. They made intercession on behalf of the eleven Marlborough Indians, that were now on their trial, and of whom I have before

---

* The same who was killed by the Indians afterwards, 27th June, 1689, in his own garrison-house at Dover, N. H. See Belknap's *History of New Hampshire*, (Farmer's ed.)

† On his return after the war, he called on the Rev. Mr. Fisk of Chelmsford, and, among other inquiries, wished to know whether Chelmsford had suffered much during the war; and being informed that it had not, and that God should be thanked for it, Wannalanset replied, "Me next." — Allen's *History of Chelmsford.*

‡ Beginning of July.　　　§ The same as Punkapog, Stoughton.

‖ Part of Woodstock.

spoken, alleging they were not guilty of the fact charged upon them. The Commissioners were not long before they issued matters with them, and sent them away.

About this time, two of those fifteen Indians brought down prisoners with the rest from Marlborough, viz. Abraham Spene and John Choo, persons that were not accused of any crime, but belonged to Natick, and were accidentally at Marlborough when the rest were seized, and so brought down for company, and held in prison some weeks, but are now released at the intercession of some of their friends, and sent out of Boston in the evening, and conducted, by Deacon Parke of Roxbury, to Mr. Elliot's house, by order of the Council, that so they might go home to Natick. But when some of the disorderly rout in Boston heard of their release, about thirty boys and young fellows got together, and repaired to the house of one of the captains* in Boston, (whom they apprehended to be no well-willer to the praying Indians,) earnestly soliciting him to head them, and go to the prison, and break it open, and take out the Indian prisoners of Marlborough and kill them, least they should be released, as two of them were this evening, as they understood. But the captain was so prudent as to deny their request, and to check them for their motion, and presently dismissed them informing authority thereof, so there was no further stir in it.† Those two Indians that were released were honest and sober Christians and had committed no offence, nor were at all accused, yet were brought to prison and tied by the neck to the rest, and put to great sufferings by many days' imprisonment in a nasty place.

About this time, [Sept. 14, 1675,] a person named Shattock of Watertown, that was a sergeant under Captain Beers, when the said Beers was slain near Squakeage,‡ had escaped very narrowly but a few days before; and being newly returned home, this man being at Charlestown in Mr. Long's porch at the sign of the Three Cranes, divers persons of quality being present, particularly Capt. Lawrence Hammond,§ the Captain of the

---

* Captain James Oliver. See note, p. 459.

† The account, given by the author of the "Letter to London," of this affair, differs materially, as will be seen by reference to a previous note, (p. 459.)

‡ Northfield.

§ Dr. Belknap, *Hist. N. H.*, page 79, *note*, (Farmer's ed.), mentions "a MS. journal, found in Prince's collection, and supposed to have been written by Captain Lawrence Hammond of Charlestown."

town, and others, this Shattock was heard to say words to this effect. "I hear the Marlborough Indians in prison in Boston, and upon trial for their lives, are like to be cleared by the court; for my part, said he, I have been lately abroad in the country's service, and have ventured my life for them, and escaped very narrowly; but if they clear those Indians, they shall hang me up by the neck before I ever serve them again." Within a quarter of an hour after these words were spoken, this man was drowned passing the ferry between Charlestown and Boston; the ferry-boat being loaded with horses, and the wind high, the boat sunk; and though there were several other men in the boat and several horses, yet all escaped with life, but this man only. I might here mention several other things of remark, that happened to other persons that were filled with displeasure and animosity against the poor Christian Indians, but shall forbear lest any be offended.

About ten days before this, a party of men, about one hundred, under command of one Capt. Gorham,* of Plymouth Colony, and Lieut. Upham of Massachusetts, being sent into the Nipmuck country, to destroy the enemies' cornfields that they had deserted, and to hinder their relief thereby in winter; these soldiers being cautioned by their instructions not to spoil any thing belonging to the poor Christian Indians, that lived among us, and had deserted their plantations of Hassanamset, Manchauge, and Chobonakonkon, three villages that lay next the English, in the Nipmuck country. But this prohibition notwithstanding, at their return, which was about the 4th of October, and as I was certainly informed that all they did in this enterprise, was to destroy much of the corn, and burn the wigwams, and mats, and other things that they found in those three villages, that belonged to our praying Indians; but the other places of Pakachooge,† Wabaage,‡ and others where there was abundance of corn, they left untouched, which after, in the winter, afforded relief to the enemy. But the praying Indians had theirs destroyed, and were the sufferers in this affair.

About the middle of October, 1675, the General Court then

* The same probably, who was one of the captains in the Narraganset fight, 19th Dec. 1675, and who fell sick and died, from the severity of the season, as is supposed.
† In Worcester and Ward.
‡ Same as Quabaog, or Brookfield.

468

sitting at Boston, there were vigorous endeavours set a foot in the Deputies' house, occasioned by petitions and complaints presented to them, from and of the people, for removing the praying Indians from their plantations ; but where to dispose them was not so duly considered. Hereupon a bill was offered to the house of magistrates about this matter; but after some debate upon the bill, not knowing well how or where to dispose these Indians, the bill was laid aside. But this demur upon the bill rather heightened an earnest pressing of it, whereupon a committee of both houses were chosen to consider of the matter. The committee met, and they were presented with a paper containing seven heads, showing the difficulty and inconvenience in that affair, and how it deserved a very serious and deliberate consideration ; the first taken from our covenant with our King, in our charter, to use our best endeavours to communicate the Christian religion to the Indians ; in pursuance whereof, there were some ministers encouraged to gain their language, and labor amongst them to that end, and had now for above thirty years' space preached the Gospel to them. 2dly. The Bible and divers other pious books were translated into their language, which divers of them could well read and understand. 3dly. A school or college built of brick, at Cambridge, at the charge of the Right Honorable Corporation in London. 4thly. Churches and Church officers are settled among them. 5thly. Divers are baptized, both men, women, and children. 6thly. In judgment of charity, several of them are believers. A second head, taken from a covenant made with those Indians and their predecessors, about thirty years since recorded, the General Court records of the Massachusetts, wherein the Indians' subjection and the English protection is mutually agreed. Now a covenant, though made with the Gibeonites, is a very binding thing, and the breach of it sorely punished by the Lord, as may appear in 2 Sam. xxi. 1, 2, 3. A third consideration, taken from our laws, which carefully provides for the encouragement and security of the praying Indians ; see the law, title *Indians*, page 74. A fourth reason, taken from the many public letters and printed papers sent from New England under a stamp of authority, both from the Commissioners of the United Colonies to the Honorable Corporation at London, and from the General Court, declaring the good success of the Gospel among them, particularly to mention only that passage in the address and petition of the General Court,

sitting at Boston, in New England, to the high and mighty
Prince, Charles the Second, and presented to his most gracious
notice, Feb. 11th, 1660, in page 7, line 25th. "Royal Sir;
If, according to our humble petition and good hope in the God
of the spirits of all flesh, the Father of mercies (who comforteth
the abject) shall make the permission of that all for which we
have and do suffer the loss of all, precious, yea, so precious in
his sight, as that your royal heart shall be inclined to show unto
us that kindness of the Lord in your Majesty's protection of us
in those liberties for which we hither came, and which hitherto
we have enjoyed, upon Hezekiah speaking comfortably to us
as to sons, this orphan shall not continue fatherless, but
grow up as a received infant under its nursing father. These
Churches shall be comforted in a door of hope opened by so
signal a pledge of the lengthening of their tranquillity. These
poor naked Gentiles, not a few of whom through Grace are
come and coming in, shall still see their wonted teachers with
encouragement of a more plentiful increase of the kingdom of
Christ among them. And the blessing of your poor afflicted
(and yet we hope, trusting in God) shall come upon the head
and heart of that great King who was sometimes in exile, as
we are. With a religious restipulation of our prayers we (prostrate at your royal feet) beg pardon for this our boldness,
craving finally that our names may be enrolled amongst your
Majesty's most humble subjects and supplicants.
            "JOHN ENDICOT, Governor.
    "In the name and with the consent of the Gen'l Court."
In this passage we see what sense the General Court had in
those times of this work among the Christian Indians. A fifth
consideration taken from an act of Parliament to encourage this
work, which is confirmed by our gracious King since his happy
restoration, wherein he hath by royal charter made to the Right
Honorable Corporation residing in London; whereby considerable sums of money were raised, and revenues purchased, and
moneys transmitted annually to encourage teachers, school-
masters, and divers other occasions for promoting the Gospelizing and civilizing these poor natives. 6thly. The General
Court hath granted those Indians lands and townships, and
thereby confirmed and settled them therein as the English;
so that, besides their own natural right, they have this legal
title, and stand possessed of them as the English are. A
seventh and last reason, taken from the constant faithfulness of

the generality of these Indians to the English, and their interest
in all changes for above thirty years' experience and servicea-
bleness in the war, when they were employed and trusted,
wherein some lost their lives and others their limbs. Now
against all these reasons (in an hour of temptation) to do any
precipitate action, referring to these Christian Indians, that hath
a tendency to frustrate and overthrow this great and good work
of Gospelizing and encouraging these Indians, would (in all
probability) reflect greatly upon the piety and prudence of the
government of New England. This paper, containing those
arguments, being offered to the committee of the General Court
for consideration, they could not deny but the matter was
weighty, and said that they intended not to present unto the
General Court any thing crossing these things; but only for
present, to satisfy the clamors of the people, to remove these
Indians from their plantations to some other places, for the
security of English and Indians also. The result was, that
the committee presented to the Court for consideration, that
those Indians of Natick be removed to Cambridge neck of land;
Wamesitt Indians to Noddle's Island; Nashobah Indians to
Concord; Hassanamesit, Magunkog, and Marlborough Indians
to Mendon; Punkapog Indians to Dorchester neck of land.
But all this signified nothing, for the English inhabitants of
those places utterly refused to admit them to live so near them;
and therefore the Court declined to consent to the committee's
proposals. And therefrom the Court steered another course;
as will appear afterward. Some persons were much offended
at the paper presented to the committee concerning the Indians,
and said the author of it was more a friend to the Indians than
the English; but 't is no strange thing for men's reason to be
darkened, if not almost lost, when the mists of passion and
temptation do prevail.

About the 18th of this instant October, John Watson, of
Cambridge (before mentioned,) Guardian to the Indians at
Natick, presented a petition to the General Court in the name,
and on behalf of those Indians; wherein they do, with great
modesty and humility, prostrate themselves at the feet of
the honored General Court, desiring they would not harbour
any jealous or harsh thoughts of them, or hearken to any false
informations against them; humbly desiring the Court to send
some more English to reside with them to inspect their
conversation, and secure them; and not to fetch them off

from their dwellings, which would expose them, especially
the aged and weak, to very much sorrow and misery, both for
want of food and apparel, especially considering that the winter was approaching. But rather, if the Court pleased, they
would deliver some of their principal men for hostages for
their fidelity, professing their innocency and integrity both to
the interest of God and the English.

But this petition obtained no favorable aspect, but rather
he that presented it was frowned upon by some. Upon the
19th day of October, the Court past an order to send troopers
to fetch down all the Wammesitt and Pakemitt* Indians; this
was suddenly done, and, to be feared, in a hurry of temptation.
The reason of this sudden motion, as I was informed, was a
report brought to the Court that a haystack, belonging to
Lieut. James Richardson of Chelmsford, was set on fire and
burnt the day before. This fact was charged upon some of the
Indians of Wamesit; but they were innocent, as was afterwards
cleared; for some skulking Indians of the enemy, that formerly
lived about Groton, the principal whereof was named Nathaniel,
he and his party did this and other mischief afterward, in burning several houses at Chelmsford. And one principal design
of the enemy was to begin a difference between the English
and praying Indians living at Wamesit, that so they might
either be secured by the English or necessitated to fly to the
enemy. This Nathaniel was afterward taken at Cochecho,
and executed at Boston, who confessed the same. Moreover,
Lieutenant Richardson, whose hay was burnt, was a person
well beloved of those Indians at Wamesit and their great
friend, who did not apprehend (as he told me) that any of
the Wamesit men had burnt his hay. But others were of a
contrary mind, willing to give credit to any report against the
praying Indians, and accordingly, by their solicitations to the
General Court, obtained an order for a troop of horse (as I said
before) to march up to Wamesit, and bring down those
Indians of Wamesit, to Boston. This matter might have been
accomplished as well by two men as forty troopers; for the
Indians, upon the least message by the Court, would readily
have obeyed.

Upon the 20th of October, Mr. Joseph Cook of Cambridge
was sent down (by Cornet Oakes, that commanded the troops,)

---

* Stoughton.

unto the Court to inform them the Wamesitt Indians were
upon the way coming down to order, and that they might be
there on the morrow; withall he acquainted the Court that
they were in number about one hundred and forty-five
men, women, and children, whereof about thirty-three were
men that were all unarmed; that many of them were naked,
and several of them decrepid with age, sundry infants, and
all wanted supplies of food, for they were fain to leave most
they had behind them, except some small matters they carried
upon their backs. Upon this information, the Court took
the matter into more deliberate consideration, and sent back
Mr. Cook, with order to return all the women, and children,
and old men back to their place, and to bring down only
the able men; which order was put into execution accordingly.

And for the praying Indians belonging to Punkapog, which
were by order brought down to Dorchester from their fort
town, by Capt. Brattle and his troops, the Court (after they
had spoken with William Ahaton* and others of their principal
men) received such satisfaction from them, that they were all
returned back to their habitations, except three or four men
that were suspected. But the Wamesit men, about thirty-three,
were brought down to Charlestown, and secured in the town-
house several days, until the Court had leisure to examine
them, and afterward the most of them were returned home
again, some persons suspected being garbled from the rest.

Upon the 26th of October, new clamors and reports were
raised and fomented against the Christian Indians of Natick,
upon pretence that some of them had fired a house or old barn
at Dedham, (a poor old house not worth ten shillings, that stood
alone far distant from the dwelling-houses.) This house, in all
probability, was set on fire a purpose by some that were back
friends to those poor Indians; thereby to take an occasion to
procure the removal of all those Indians from Natick; the con-
trivers whereof well knew that the magistrates generally were
very slow to distrust those poor Christians, this artifice was
therefore used to provoke them. God (who knows all) will I
hope one day awaken and convince the consciences of those
persons that have been industriously active to traduce and afflict
those poor innocent Christians, without cause; for, as to the
body of them, they were always true and faithful to the
English; and I never saw or heard any substantial evidence to

* A name variously written, and very often beginning with an N.
He was son of Tahattawan, Sachem of Musketaquid, since Concord.

the contrary. Besides this of burning the house, there were other false informations presented at the same time to the General Court, to stir them up to a sharp procedure against those Indians; but the authors of those things being slain, I shall omit to mention them.

This contrivance against the Natick Indians obtained that which it was designed for, viz. the passing an order in the General Court, forthwith to remove them from their place unto Deer Island; having first obtained the consent of Mr. Samuel Shrimpton, of Boston, (in whose possession that Island was,) to place them there at present, with this prohibition, that they should not cut down any growing wood, nor do any damage to his sheep kept there. In pursuance of this order, Capt. Thomas Prentiss, (who was a person civil and friendly to those Indians,) with a party of horse, was commanded to bring them down speedily to a place called the Pines,* upon Charles River, about two miles above Cambridge, where boats were appointed to be in readiness to take them on board, and take them to the aforesaid Island. Captain Prentiss accordingly went up to Natick, with a few men and five or six carts, to carry such things as were of greatest necessity; and he declared to them the Court's pleasure for their removal, unto which they quietly and readily submitted, and came down with him at an hour or two warning, about two hundred souls of all sorts. There was one family of them, about twelve in number, the principal man named old Jethro,† with his sons and relations, who secretly ran away in the night; but this man and his relations were not praying Indians, nor did they live at Natick, only since the wars, but dwelt at a place near Sudbury, Nobscot hill, and never submitted to the Christian profession, but separated from them, being sons of ill fame, and especially the old man, who had the repute to be a powow; those ran away for fear at this time, and were with the enemy, but were taken afterwards at Cocheco, and hanged at Boston. Good Mr. Elliot, that faithful instructor and teacher of the praying Indians, met them at the place before mentioned, where they were to be embarked, who comforted and encouraged and instructed and prayed with them, and for them; exhorting them to patience in their suffer-

---

* Probably near the present site of the United States Arsenal.

† *Tantamous* was his Indian name.—See Shattuck's *History of Concord.*

ings, and confirming the hearts of those disciples of Christ; and exhorting them to continue in the faith, for through many tribulations we must enter into the kingdom of heaven. There were some other Englishmen at the place called the Pines with Mr. Elliot, who were much affected in seeing and observing how submissively and Christianly and affectionately those poor souls carried it, seeking encouragement, and encouraging and exhorting one another with prayers and tears at the time of the embarkment, being, as they told some, in fear that they should never return more to their habitations, but be transported out of the country; of this I was informed by eye and ear witnesses of the English nation that were upon the place at the time. In the night, about midnight, the tide serving, being the 30th of October, 1675, those poor creatures were shipped in three vessels and carried away to Deer Island above mentioned, which was distant from that place about four leagues, where I shall leave them at present.

Upon the same day that the order past to remove those native Indians to Deer Island, the Wamesit Indians before mentioned being in prison at Charlestown, thirty-three men were sent for before the General Court at Boston, and charged with burning a stack of hay at Chelmsford, belonging to James Richardson. The Indians were first examined singly and apart, and then more of them together, but they all vehemently denied the fact or privity with any that did it; but, notwithstanding, they were sorely taunted at with bitter words by some that accused them; but no proof appeared, and it was afterward discovered that they were all innocent, and that the enemy did it as I have before related; the issue of this examination and charge was, that three of the company, viz. one named Will Hawkins, a Narragansett Indian, that used constantly to work about Salem, and was now, since the war, retired to Wamesit, and two others that were not praying Indians, nor properly belonging to Wamesit, but retired thither since the war; these three were condemned to be sold for slaves, and sent out of the country, and accordingly committed to prison in order to their disposal out of the country; and afterward were sent away. But all the rest, being thirty, were ordered to return back to Charlestown to continue under restraint still. A vote passed in the House of Deputies, as I heard, finding all the Wamesitt Indians guilty of burning the hay; but it was not consented unto by the magistrates, and so, after the adjournment of the

Court, the Council ordered the taking out of some of the most suspicious Indians from the Wamesits, who did not properly belong to them, but were come in to them since the war; these being garbled out and secured in prison. The rest of the Wamesit Indians, being about twenty, were sent back to their wives and children at Wamesit. But as they passed home, being under the guard of Lieutenant James Richardson, and a file of soldiers, they were to march through a village called Woburn, at which time the trained band of that place were exercising. Lieutenant Richardson and his Indians, with their guard, before they drew near the English soldiers, made halt, and he held out his handkerchief as a flag of truce, whereupon the Captain and officers of the band sent to Richardson, who showing them his commission from the Council to conduct those Indians safely to their homes; whereupon the Captain and officers gave very strict charge to all the soldiers not to shoot a gun until all the Indians were past and clear, nor yet to give any opprobrious words. But notwithstanding this strict prohibition, when the Indians were passing by, a young fellow, a soldier named Knight, discharged his musket and killed one of the Indians stone dead, being very near him. The person slain was a stout young man, very nearly allied to the principal praying Indians of Natick and Wamesit, whose grandfather and uncle were pious men, his father long since slain in the war with the Magues. The murderer was presently apprehended and committed to prison, and not long after tried for his life, but was acquitted by the jury, much contrary to the mind of the bench; the jury alleged they wanted evidence, and the prisoner plead that his gun went off by accident, indeed witnesses were mealy-mouthed in giving evidence. The jury was sent out again and again by the judges, who were much unsatisfied with the jury's proceedings; but yet the jury did not see cause to alter their mind, and so the fellow was cleared.

About the beginning of November, intelligence came from Mendon, by two of the principal Christian Indians that escaped, viz. James Speen and Job Kattenanit, how the enemy had seized upon, and carried away captive, the Christian Indians that were at Hassanamesit, who were gathering, threshing, and putting up in Indian barns (as the manner is) a considerable crop of Indian corn that grew in that place and parts adjacent; these two men, and some squaws and children, being at a little distance from the rest, made a shift to get away, but could not certainly relate what number of the enemy there were, or whither they had carried their friends. The people captivated were for the most part unarmed, about fifty men, and one hundred and fifty women and children; the enemy's Indians, as we afterwards particularly understood, were about three hundred, all well armed, who declared to our Christian Indians, (among whom they had some kindred,) and wanted them to go with them quietly, then they would spare their lives; otherwise they would take away all their corn, and then they would be famished. And further they argued with them, if we do not kill you, and that you go to the English again, they will either force you all to some Island as the Natick Indians are, where you will be in danger to be starved with cold and hunger, and most probably in the end be all sent out of the country for slaves. These kind of arguments used by the enemy, and our friends' inability to defend themselves, together with their fear of hard measure from the English, whereof some of them had late experience; for among these were the eleven Indians that were so long imprisoned at Boston, and tried for their lives upon a pretended murder done by them at Lancaster above mentioned, whereof they knew themselves innocent, and were acquitted; but they smarted so much, in and about the matter, they were in fear of further sufferings; upon these considerations, many of them at last were inclined, in this strait, of two evils to choose the least, as it to them appeared, and to accompany the enemy to their quarters, under their promise of good usage and protection; and perhaps if Englishmen, and good Christians too, had been in their case and under like temptations, possibly they might have done as they did.

The chief man among these praying Indians, who also was their ruler, named Capt. Tom, *alias* Wuttasacomponom,* a prudent, and I believe, a pious man, and had given good demonstration of it many years. I had particular acquaintance with him, and cannot in charity think otherwise concerning him in his life, or at his death, though possibly in this action he was tempted beyond his strength; for, had he done as he ought, he should rather have suffered death, than have gone

* He was taken 9th June, and after lying in prison in Boston until the 22d following, was hanged, and another at the same time. One of our anonymous authors remarks; "They both died (as is to be hoped) penitent, praying to God, not like the manner of the heathen."

among the wicked enemies of the people of God. This man yielded to the enemies' arguments, and by his example drew most of the rest, for which he afterwards suffered death, being executed at Boston, the June after; yet there were some of those Christian Indians went away with the enemy with heavy hearts and weeping eyes, particularly Joseph Tuckappawill,* the pastor of the church at Hassanamesitt, and his aged father, Naoas, and some others, of which I had particular information from some that were eye and ear witnesses thereof. This providence, concerning those Christian Indians being carried thus away by the enemy, was a very deep wound to the work of Gospelizing the Indians, for this people were considerable for number as before is hinted. Being the greatest part of three Indian villages, viz. Hassanamesit, Magunkog, and Chobone-Konhonom.† It was also a weakening to the English in removing these frontier Indian plantations and forts, which would have been as walls under God to us, as the sequel proved. Besides, many of these poor Christians lost their lives by war, sickness, and famine; and some were executed that came in to us: it was a great scandal to the Christian religion they professed, yet through God's favor some of them were preserved alive and are reconciled again to the English, and now live among the rest of the Christian Indians, and in especial those of them that lamented and mourned when they were carried away; the Lord spared their lives and brought them back to the enjoyment of sanctuary mercies.

Upon this intelligence of the enemies' appearance about Hassanamesit, two companies of English soldiers were despatched away into these parts, one commanded by Captain Daniel Henchman, the other by Captain Joseph Sill. This last took with him for guides five Natick Indians. When they came to Hassanamesit, they found signs of the enemy, but could see no considerable company of them. But Captain Syll, being at Hassanamesit the 6th of November, hearing a noise early in the morning, sent forth two files of men, with two Indians, viz. James Quanapohit, and Eliazor Pegin; they had not gone far, but they discovered seven of the enemy and one of them leading an Englishman; the enemy discovering

---

* Hutchinson (from Mr. Eliot) writes the name of this Indian *Tuppuk-koowelin.* The Apostle considered him a sound and godly man.

† In Dudley. Spelt in another page *Chobonokonomum.*

our men fled, but the two Indians James and Eliazor pursued them so close, and firing upon the man that led the English youth, he was forced to leave his prisoner, and they rescued him and brought him to their captain; * also James the Indian recovered a musket from the enemy at the same time; this English youth, whose name was Christopher Muchin, was thus delivered from the barbarous enemy by the courage and activity of our Indians. This English so taken informed the Captain that those seven Indians with whom he was taken had seized him at Peter Bent's mill in Marlborough the day before, and had also seized and scalped a youth of about nine years old, that was his master Peter Bent's son, and left the lad at the mill as dead. Another good service that one of those Christian Indians did in this expedition, namely Thomas Quannapohit, (brother to James above mentioned,) this man had the use of his left hand only, for he lost the use of his other hand by a gun-shot in the beginning of the war at Mount Hope, as is before related. This fellow was witty and courageous, as may appear in the story following. After the former service done at Hassanemesit, the two English companies joined with Captain Daniel Henchman and Captain Joseph Syll. And after their conjunction they marched to a place called Packachooge, about ten miles distant from Hassanamesit towards the northwest, where was great plenty of good Indian corn, and in this place hoped to meet some of the enemy: coming to this place, they saw signs of Indians that had been lately there, but it seems were withdrawn upon the approach of the English. At this place our forces took up their quarters one night, there being two wigwams which was good shelter for our soldiers, the weather being wet and stormy. The next morn our forces searched about the cornfields to find the enemy, but could not discover them, though in all probability the enemy saw them in all their motions and concealed themselves; for this is their ordinary way, to lie hid in thick swamps and other secret places, and to move as our men do scatter themselves in small parties, and lie close observing all our men's motions. The English in their search found above

---

* "When our army marched to Wachusett, and a soldier was ready to shoot at three Indians, a child with them in the habit of an Indian papoos, the child at the very instant crying out he was an English boy, the soldier forbore to shoot, and so the child ran to the English and escaped." — MS. Narrative, Rev. T. Cobbet.

one hundred bushels of Indian corn newly gathered, and a great quantity of corn standing. About ten o'clock in the forenoon, the English captains and their soldiers marched back to Hassanamesit; being gone about two miles on their way, Captain Henchman missing, as he apprehended, his letter-case, wherein his writings and orders were, he sent back two Englishmen and the Indian Thomas on horseback, to see at the wigwams where he lodged to find his papers. These messengers accordingly going back, the Indian led them away and ascending up a steep hill, at the top whereof stood the wigwam; as soon as ever he discovered it, being not above six rods distance, he saw two Indian enemies standing at the wigwam door, newly come out, and four more sitting at the fire in the house; at which sight he bestirred himself, and looking back called earnestly (as if many men were behind coming up the hill) to hasten away and encompass the enemy; one of the enemy thereupon presented his gun at our Indian, but the gun missing fire, (probably the moist rainy weather had put it out of case,) whereupon the rest of them that were in the wigwam came all out and ran away as fast as they could, suspecting that the English forces were at hand; and then Thomas with his two comrades, having thus prudently scared away the enemy, they thought it seasonable also to ride back again to their company as fast as they could. And indeed there was good reason for it, because Thomas the Indian had only a pistol, one of the Englishmen, who was their chirurgeon, a young man, had no gun; the third had a gun, but the flint was lost: so that they were in ill case to defend themselves or offend the enemy; but God preserved them by the prudence and courage of this Indian, which deliverance one of the Englishmen directly acknowledged to me, attributing their preservation under God to this fellow. So they got safe to their Captain, who in the interim searching diligently had found his letter-case, and staid for these messengers; so that God ordered this affair to magnify his own grace in delivering those men, and to give to the English a demonstration of the fidelity and prudence of our Christian Indians.

Notwithstanding these signal services performed by these our Indian friends, yet there were some of Capt. Syll's inferior officers and soldiers, who (being infected with the spirit of enmity against all Indians) murmured greatly against these Indians, their guides and keepers, in so much that their Captain (to satisfy them) sent home three of the five, though, as he told me, he found no fault with them, but did it merely to quiet his soldiers that were of malevolent spirits against them; he retained with him James and Thomas Quannapohit till his return. After this, nothing was done against the enemy by these two companies; only Capt. Henchman, after Syll and he were parted, having no Indian guide with him, sustained a great loss; for his lieutenant, one Philip Curtis, of Roxbury, a stout man, was slain, and another private soldier with him; and the Captain in great danger, in a charge that Capt. Henchman and a small party of his men made in the night upon some Indians, judged to be about forty, that were in a wigwam at Hassanamesit, which enterprise was a few days after the parting of their forces. Capt. Henchman told me he judged several of the enemy were slain in the wigwam by him attacked, but the certainty is not known. But 't was certain he lost two of his men as before said, whereof his Lieutenant was one; whose heads the enemy cut off, and placed upon a crotched pole at the wigwam door, faced against each other, which were seen a few days after by the English.*

About the 13th of November, one of our Christian Indians, (a trusty and faithful man,) named Job Kattenanit, who had been preacher at Magunkog, this man having three children carried away by the enemy from Hassanamesit, (the story whereof is formerly mentioned,) himself at that time escaping to the English at Mendon; he applied himself to Major Gookin, desiring of him a pass to go into the woods to seek for his children, and endeavour to get them out of the enemies' hand; alleging that his affections were so great to his children, (their mother being dead,) and he in a widowed estate, was willing to venture his life among the enemy, in order to the recovery of his children (and possibly, said he, if God spare my life, I may bring you some intelligence of the residence and state of the enemy, which may be very useful to the English). These arguments prevailed with the Major (who had also special order from the Council to endeavour to gain intelligence of the enemy) to grant a pass or certificate to the said Job, in the words following. " These may certify that the bearer hereof, Job, of Magunkog, is a trusty Indian, and therefore, if any Englishman meet him, it is desired they will not misuse him,

---

* See Hubbard's *Narrative*, p. 45.

but secure him, and convey him to the Governor or myself, and they shall be satisfied for their pains.

"Dated the 13th day of the 9th month, 1675.

(Signed) "DANIEL GOOKIN, Sen."

The design of this certificate was innocent, and more respected the Indian's safe conduct at his return, than to secure him at his forth going. But it met with hard construction, and the person that had it, with much sufferings; and, consequently, the projection to gain intelligence of the state of the enemy was frustrated, which was a matter the English greatly needed at this time, being inland with a great expedition against the enemy. The providence of God so ordered this matter, that this Job, at his going forth, met with some of Capt. Henchman's scouts, not far from Hassanamesit, whom the Indian saw before they discovered him, and he could easily have concealed himself, (as he told me,) but he, not fearing to speak with the English, from whom he was sent with a pass, stood in open view; and when the English saw him, they rode up to him, and some of them said, "Let us kill him"; but others said, "He is a lone man, let us not kill him, but carry him to our captain to be examined." This latter counsel prevailed; and then they seized him, and disarmed him, and took away his clothes, so that his gun and some clothes were then plundered, and he never had them again to this day. So they carried him to Capt. Henchman, who examined him, for the Indian spoke good English; the Indian told him all the truth of matters, and showed him his certificate; but the Captain, being ignorant of the design, sent both him and his pass to the Governor, at Boston, who more to satisfy the clamors of the people than for any offence committed by this man, he was committed to the common jail, and there remained under very great sufferings for three weeks' time; for there were many Indians there, in a small prison, which was very noisome. After three weeks' time, when the clamor was over, he was discharged from prison, and sent to Deer Island, unto the rest of his suffering countrymen. He had committed no offence (that ever I heard of), but was imprisoned merely to still the clamors of the people, who railed much against this poor fellow, and fain would have had him put to death, (though they knew not wherefore.) But those murmurings were not only against the Indian, but as much against Major Gookin, who granted him the certificate; some not sparing to say, that he was sent forth to give intelligence to the enemy, and such like false and reproachful reflections upon their friends, that had many ways approved their fidelity to the country. But this was an hour of temptation and murmuring, as sometime God's own people are inclinable unto, as at Massah and Meribah. Thus it pleased God to exercise this poor Job, yet reserved him for greater service afterward, as in the sequel will appear.

The 15th of November, there befell another great trial to the poor praying Indians at Wamesit; they lived very near to Lieutenant Thomas Henchman, about two miles from Chelmsford, and were under the guard and care of Lieutenant Richardson, appointed thereunto by the Council. The antecedents to this affliction of the Indians was this. A barn belonging to Richardson, being full of hay and corn, was set on fire and consumed. This was done by some skulking rogues of the enemy, that formerly lived about Groton, as we afterward understood; but the English at Chelmsford imputed the fact to the Wamesitt Indians, as they had formerly done by the same man's hay, and thereby brought much trouble upon these poor Christians. Upon this occasion, about fourteen armed men from Chelmsford, pretending to scout and look out for the enemy, but as I was informed, it was moved among them and concluded, that they would go to the wigwams of the Wamesit Indians, their neighbours, and kill them all; in pursuance whereof they came to the wigwams, and called to the poor Indians to come out of doors, which most of them readily did, both men, women, and children, not in the least suspecting the English would hurt them. But two of the English being loaded with pistol-shot, being not far off, fired upon them and wounded five women and children, and slew outright a lad of about twelve years old, which child's mother was also one of the wounded; she was a widow, her name Sarah, a woman of good report for religion. She was daughter to a Sagamor, named Sagamor John, who was a great friend to the English, who lived and died at the same place. Her two husbands, both deceased, were principal Sagamores, the one named John Tohatooner, and the other Oonamog, both pious men, and rulers of the praying Indians, one at Marlborough, the other at Nashobah; her last husband died before the war, the first long before. This youth slain was only son to the first husband; his grandfather, old Tahattawarre,* was a Sachem, and a pious man. God was pleased to restrain the other twelve Englishmen, that they did not fire their guns upon

---

* This was the distinguished Sachem of Concord. His name is sometimes spelled *Attawan, Attawance, Tahattance.* This family were among the most distinguished Christian Indians. — See Shattuck's *Hist. of Concord.*

the poor Indians; that which was done was too much, and was an action very much decried by all wise and prudent men, especially by the magistracy and ministry. As soon as this intelligence came to Authority, warrants were sent forth to apprehend the murderers; their names were Lorgin and Robins; they were seized and committed to prison, and afterward tried for their lives, but were cleared by the jury, to the great grief and trouble generally of magistracy and ministry and other wise and godly men. The jury pretended want of clear evidence; but some feared it was rather a mist of temptation and prejudice against these poor Indians that darkened their way. This cruel murder and fight occasioned most of those poor Christian Indians to fly away from their wigwams not long after, but carried little or nothing with them; but for fear, rather exposed themselves and families to the hardships and sufferings of hunger and cold, than to be under the harsh dealings of cruel men. But as soon as the Council were informed that the Indians were fled, they sent out orders to Lieutenant Henchman to send after them, and endeavour to persuade them to return; but their fears so prevailed that they refused to return, but sent back a letter directed

" *To* Mr. THOMAS HENCHMAN, *of Chelmsford.*

" I, Numphow, and John a Line, we send the messenger to
" you again (*Wecoposit*) with this answer, we cannot come
" home again, we go towards the French, we go where Wan-
" nalansit is; the reason is, we went away from our home, we
" had help from the Council, but that did not do us good, but
" we had wrong by the English. 2dly. The reason is we went
" away from the English, for when there was any harm done in
" Chelmsford, they laid it to us and said we did it, but we know
" ourselves we never did harm to the English, but we go away
" peaceably and quietly. 3dly. As for the Island, we say there
" is no safety for us, because many English be not good, and
" may be they come to us and kill us, as in the other case.
" We are not sorry for what we leave behind, but we are sorry
" the English have driven us from our praying to God and from
" our teacher. We did begin to understand a little of praying
" to God. We thank humbly the Council. We remember
" our love to Mr. Henchman and James Richardson.

" The mark of £ JOHN LYNE, } their Rulers."
" The mark of ⊅ NUMPHOW,* }

* Numphow was a very considerable man among the Wamesits. Two of his sons joined the enemy, who, on submitting again to the English, barely escaped with their lives. — See *Book of the Indians.*

This is a true copy of their letter, word for word, wherein may be seen, that they had reason as well as fear, that put them upon that motion. This letter was brought back by the messenger sent after them, an Indian, named Wepocositt, that was servant to William Fletcher, of Chelmsford, whom Lieutenant Henchman procured to go after them. About twenty-three days after this, the greatest part of the Wamesit Indians (being put to great straits for want of food) returned back to their wigwams, whereof Lieutenant Henchman forthwith informed the Council at Boston; and they gave him order to encourage and cherish them, and also appointed a committee, viz. Major Gookin, Major Willard, and Mr. John Elliot, to ride up to Chelmsford to encourage and settle them, and to persuade the English at Chelmsford to be more friendly to them, also to take care for necessary provision for them; moreover, the same committee were appointed to visit the Nashobah Christian Indians that now lived at Concord, and to endeavour to quiet and compose the minds of the English there, touching those Indians.

In pursuance whereof, the said committee, (in a cold and very sharp season,) upon Dec. 13th, went up to those places to put the Council's order in execution, which was done accordingly, and matters were so well settled, (as they conceived,) that those poor Indians were in hopes to live quietly. The said committee also sent forth some of the Indians to fetch back eighteen of the Wamesit Indians that were left behind, being afraid to return with the rest, but staid about Pennagog; among whom was that poor widow who was wounded and her son slain by the Chelmsford men, before mentioned; those came to the rest a few days after. The committee also appointed Englishmen to be as guardians to those Indians by night and day, to prevent any inconvenience either to the English or Indians; and for the Christian Indians that were at Concord, the committee placed them under the inspection and government of Mr. John Hoare;* the said Indians having pitched their wigwams in his ground, near his house, this man was very loving to them, and very diligent and careful to promote their good, and to secure the English from any fear or damage by them. But notwithstanding the care of the Council, and the travel of

---

* This gentleman was one of those whom prejudice did not blind. He was of Concord, and died 2 April, 1701. He was one of the original purchasers of that town. He removed from Scituate to Concord in 1659 or 1660. — Deane's *History of Scituate*, p. 285.

this committee for the settling this affair, yet new troubles
arose not long after this, through the inordinate fears and
corruptions of men ; which in the sequel may be further declared. One thing more I shall here add, which was told me
by Mr. Thomas Clark, preacher at Chelmsford, concerning
those Wamesit Indians ; he, speaking with the teacher of those
Indians, named Symon Beckom,* had this account from him.
At their return, being questioned by Mr. Clark what they did
in their absence, said Symon, "We kept three Sabbaths in the
woods ; the first Sabbath," said he, " I read and taught the people
out of Psalm 35, the second Sabbath from Psalm 46, the third
Sabbath out of Psalm 118," which Scriptures, being considered,
were very suitable to encourage and support them in their sad
condition ; this shows, that those poor people have some little
knowledge of, and affection to the word of God, and have some
little ability (through grace) to apply such meet portions
thereof, as are pertinent to their necessities.

1675. About the latter end of Dec., I had (among others)
sometimes opportunity to accompany Mr. Elliot to visit and
comfort the poor Christian Indians confined to Deer Island,
who were (a little before) increased to be about five hundred
souls, by addition of the Punkapog Indians, sent thither upon
as little cause as the Naticks were. The enmity, jealousy,
and clamors of some people against them put the magistracy
upon a kind of necessity to send them all to the Island ; and
although it was a great suffering to the Indians to live there,
yet God brought forth this good by it ; first, their preservation
from the fury of the people, secondly, the humbling and better-
ing the Indians by this sore affliction. I observed in all my
visits to them, that they carried themselves patiently, humbly,
and piously, without murmuring or complaining against the
English for their sufferings, (which were not few,) for they
lived chiefly upon clams and shell-fish, that they digged out of
the sand, at low water ; the Island was bleak and cold, their
wigwams poor and mean, their clothes few and thin ; some little
corn they had of their own, which the Council ordered to be
fetched from their plantations, and conveyed to them by little

---

* Sometimes written *Betokom.* He had been with the enemy, and
was pardoned. In 1685 he was among the Pennakooks, and was one of
the fifteen who petitioned governor Cranfield for protection against the
Mohawks. His name is written to that letter *Simon Detogkom.* This
letter, with three others, is appended to Belknap's *New Hampshire.*

and little ; also a boat and man was appointed to look after them. I may say in the words of truth (according to my apprehension), there appeared among them much practical Christianity in this time of their trials.

After the fight, which was between the English and the Indians at Narraganset, the 11th * day of December, 1675, the Council of Massachusetts were very desirous to use means to gain intelligence of the state of the enemy ; and, in pursuance thereof, passed an order empowering Major Gookin to use his best endeavour to procure two meet persons of the praying Indians, from Deer Island, to undertake that service, and to promise them a reward for their encouragement. Accordingly, upon the 28th of December, he went down to Deer Island, and advising with two or three of the principal men, they approved the design and of the persons he had pitched upon for that employ, if they could be procured, namely, Job Kattenanit and James Quannapohit (of whom I have formerly spoken), These, being spoken to by the Major about this matter, answered, that they were very sensible of the great hazard and danger in this undertaking ; yet their love to the English, and that they might give more demonstrations of their fidelity, they being also encouraged by their chief men, they said, by God's assistance, they would willingly adventure their lives in this service. They had no more but five pounds apiece promised for their encouragement. The same day, the Major brought them up with him, and conveyed them privately, in the night, to his house at Cambridge, and there kept them in secret until all things were fitted for their journey, and instruction and orders given them. And then, upon the 30th of December, before day, they were sent away, being conducted by an Englishman unto the falls of Charles River, and so they passed on their journey undiscovered. These two spies acquitted themselves in this service prudently, and faithfully brought the intelligence which might have conduced much to the advantage of the English had their advice been wisely improved. They first fell among the enemy's quarters about

---

* There is no difference of opinion now among historians, nor was there among those who wrote at the time, concerning the date of the memorable Swamp Fight. Not writing until the next year, Mr. Gookin probably set it down from recollection, and thus made an error of eight days.

Menumesse,* where the Nipmuck, Quabage, and Wesakam †
Indians ‡ kept their rendezvous, among whom were most of the
praying Indians that were captivated from Hassanamesit, as
was formerly declared. These spies were instructed to tell a
fair, yet true story to the enemy; that they were some of the
poor Natick Indians, confined to Deer Island, where they had
lived all this winter under great sufferings; and now these being
gotten off, they were willing to come among their countrymen
and find out their friends that had lived at Hassanamesit, and
to understand the numbers, strength, unity, and estate of their
countrymen, that were in hostility with the English, that so
they might be the better able to advise their friends at Deer
Island and elsewhere, what course to steer, for the future; and
that one of them (namely, Job) had all his children among
them, and other kindred, which induced him to run this adventure. These, and such like fair pretences, took off much
suspicion, and gave them . opportunity to inform themselves
particularly of all the affairs and designs of the enemy.

1675. Upon the 24th day of January, James Quannapohit
(one of the spies) returned, and was conducted to Major
Gookin's house, from the falls of Charles River, by one Isaac
Williams, an Englishman, that lived near that place. This man
was friendly to the Christian Indians, and had courteously entertained, lodged, and refreshed this our spy the night before; for
he was very weary, faint, and spent in travelling near eighty
miles. The snow being deep in the woods, he was necessitated to go upon rackets or snow-shoes, upon the top of the
snow, which is very tiresome travelling. His examination and
intelligence being written by Major Gookin, he went down
with him to the Governor and Council the next day. The
particulars of his examination are too long here to be mentioned, ‖ and not so pertinent to our design, though most things he
related proved true, which argued for his fidelity. The main
matters were, that the enemy quartered in several places this
winter. Philip and his soldiers not far from Fort Albany. The

---

* The name of this place is variously written. Mrs. Rowlandson
has it *Wenimesset*. It was in New Braintree. In the *Coll. Mass.
Hist. Soc.* it is spelt *Menemesseg*.

† This name, according to Roger Williams, signifies *sea*.

‡ A small tribe on the borders of Weshakom Pond, in Sterling.

‖ This valuable document is printed in 1 *Coll. Mass. Hist. Soc.*
VI. 205 *et seq.*

Nipmuck and divers others, about Menumesse. That they intended a general rendezvous in the spring of the year, and then they would prosecute the war vigorously against the English, burn and destroy the towns. They heard of the fight between the English and the Narragansetts, and rejoiced much at that breach, hoping now to be strong enough to deal with the English, when the Narragansetts and they were joined. That there were messengers sent (while our spies were there) from the Narragansetts to the Nipmucks, that quartered about Menumesse, declaring their desire to join with them and Philip. That the enemy gloried much in their number and strength, and that all this war their loss of men was inconsiderable. They seemed to be very high and resolute, and expect to carry all before them. He said, they lived this winter upon venison chiefly, and upon some corn they had got together before winter from several deserted plantations. The enemy boasted of their expectation to be supplied with arms and ammunition and men from the French, by the hunting Indians.

He declared the enemy purposed, within three weeks, to fall upon Lancaster, and cut off the bridge in the first place, to obstruct any assistance (which thing the enemy exactly fulfilled, as to time and mode of their proceeding, as this man declared). Also, successively to burn and destroy the other frontier town, which they did accordingly. The reason why this spy returned so soon, and left his comrade, was this; because Mautampe,* a chief sachem among the Quabage Indians, declared to James, that he should accompany him to visit Philip, and to acquaint and inform him of affairs at Boston, and of the breach between the English and Narragansetts. James, being a witty fellow, seemed to consent to Mautampe's desire, but withal insinuated this excuse; saith he, "Philip knows me, and that I fought against him last summer on the English part at Mount Hope, and he will not believe me, that I am really turned to his side, unless I do some notable exploit first, and kill some Englishmen and carry their heads to him. Let me, therefore, have some opportunity and time to do some signal service, before I go to Philip." This excuse seemed to satisfy Mautampe. But James, doubting that he would take him with him in the journey, (he being intended to take this journey within a

---

* This sachem fell into the hands of the English and was hanged. See *Book of the Indians*, iii. 80.

few days after), and James could not prevent it, if the sachem should change his mind and command him to accompany him ; therefore James resolved to endeavour an escape before the sachem took his journey, especially being informed secretly by Joseph Tuhapawillin, the minister of Hassenasit (there with the enemy against his mind), that Philip had given strict order to all his soldiers to surprise, as they could, certain of the praying Indians, of their most valiant men, whereof this James was one ; and that they should bring them unto him alive, that he might put them to some tormenting and cruel death ; which hitherto had been prevented by the care and kindness of a great captain among them, named John, with one eye, belonging to Nashaway, who had civilly treated and protected James, and entertained him at his wigwam all the time of his being there. The cause of this his special love to James was because he had been a fellow-soldier with him in the Manhake war, and about ten years past. James acquainted his comrade Job with his purpose to escape home, desiring his company with him. Job concealed his purpose, and secretly contrived with him for his escape ; " But," said he, " I am not yet in a posture fit to go. for I cannot carry my children with me, and I have not yet considered of a way to bring them off; moreover," said he, " I am willing to venture a little longer, and go down with the Indians that are to meet with the Narragansetts ; and, if I live, I may get more intelligence. And," said he, " if God spare my life, I intend to come away about three weeks hence." But James earnestly persuaded him to go with him now ; " for," said he, " after I am gone, I fear the enemy will suspect us to be spies, and then kill you." But Job was resolved to stay and venture a little longer, in order to his children's release, and to contrive a way for the escape of some other Christian Indians that were among the enemy, that longed for deliverance. So James came away, and got safe home as is above declared ;* but Job staid behind, and returned not until the 9th of February ; and then, about ten o'clock in the night, came to Major Gookin's house at Cambridge, conducted thither by one Joseph Miller, that lived near the falls of Charles River. He brought tidings, that before he came from the enemy at Menemesse, a

---

* " Job and he pretended to go out a hunting, killed three deer quickly, and, perceiving they were dogged by some other Indians, went over a pond and lay in a swamp till before day ; and, when they had prayed together, he run away." — *Cotton MSS.*

party of the Indians, about four hundred, were marched forth
to attack and burn Lancaster; and, on the morrow, which was
February 10th, they would attempt it. This time exactly
suited with James his information before hinted, which was
not then credited as it should have been; and, consequently, not
so good means used to prevent it, or at least to have lain in
ambushments for the enemy. As soon as Major Gookin understood this tidings by Job, he rose out of his bed, and, advising with Mr. Danforth, one of the Council, that lived near
him, they despatched away post, in the night, to Marlborough,
Concord, and Lancaster, ordering forces to surround Lancaster
with all speed. The posts were at Marlborough by break of
day, and Captain Wadsworth,* with about forty soldiers, marched away, as speedily as he could possibly, to Lancaster (which
was ten miles distant). But, before he got there, the enemy
had set fire on the bridge; but Captain Wadsworth got over,
and beat off the enemy, recovered a garrison-house that stood
near another bridge, belonging to Cyprian Stevens, and so,
through God's favor, prevented the enemy from cutting off the
garrison; God strangely preserving that handful with Captain
Wadsworth, for the enemy were numerous, about four hundred,
and lay in ambushment for him on the common road. But his
guides conducted him a private way; and so they got safe to
Cyprian Stevens his garrison as abovementioned. But the
enemy had taken and burnt another garrison-house very near
the other, only a bridge and a little ground parting them. This
house burnt was the minister's house, named Mr. Rolandson,
wherein were slain and taken captive about forty persons, the
minister's wife and children amongst them. But I must re-
collect myself; it being not my design to write of the doings
and sufferings of the English in this tract, but of the Indians,
our friends. Besides this seasonable information concerning
Lancaster, by Job, he also informed of the conjunction of the
Narragansett Indians with the other enemies, and of their further purposes shortly to attack Medfield, Groton, and Marlborough, and other places. Sundry other material things Job
informed us of, touching the Narragansetts and their designs.
Moreover, he and others (our friends among the Indians) had

---

* Captain Samuel Wadsworth, of Milton, who, in April following,
fell in Sudbury fight, with about fifty of his men. — Holmes's *Annals of
America*, I. 380. The particulars of that affair are touched upon by our
author, as will be seen further on.

contrived a way and appointed a time for the escape of his children and some honest Indians with them ; and agreed upon a place and time to meet them in the woods, that he might conduct them safe to the English; and, in special, Joseph Tuckappawillin, pastor of the church (late at Hassanesit), and his aged father, Naoas, the deacon of the church, with their wives and children, which were of that number. And for this purpose, Job made a petition to the Council to have liberty and opportunity to go at the time appointed to fetch them in, and it was granted him. But notwithstanding there were vicissitudes of intervening providence, that befell those poor Indians and Job also, before it was effected; as in that which follows will appear. After the coming back of those two spies, they were sent again to Deer Island. And although they had run such hazards, and done so good service (in the judgment of the authority of the country and other wise and prudent men), yet the vulgar spared not to load them with reproaches, and to impute the burning of Mendon (a deserted village) unto them, and to say that all they informed were lies, and that they held correspondence with the enemy, or else they had not come back safe ; and divers other things were muttered, both against the spies and authority that sent them, tending to calumniate the poor men that had undertaken and effected this great affair, which none else (but they) were willing to engage in; which declares the rude temper of those times.

About the 5th of February, a petition from the Wamesit Indians (living near Chelmsford) was presented to the Council by the hands of Jerathmel Bowers (one of their guardians), the purport whereof was, to desire earnestly that they might be removed from the place where they were; declaring they feared to stay, because (in all probability) other Indians would come and do mischief shortly, and it would be imputed to them, and they should suffer for it. The Council answered their petition, that they would endeavour to remove them speedily. But there was greater delay about it than was intended, by reason of divers other momentous occasions intervening. So that, within a few days after, these poor Indians of Wamesit (finding themselves in great danger, being threatened by some of their English neighbours,) they all ran away into the woods towards Pennahoog; only they left behind them six or seven aged persons, blind and lame, which, not long after, were destroyed by some cruel and wicked men, in a secret manner, who set fire to the wigwam where they kept, and burnt them all. The authors of this fact were not openly known, nor so clearly witnessed thereof, as to proceed against them by authority ; but two persons were suspected strongly to be the actors, one of whom shortly after was slain at Sudbury ; the other is yet alive, who, if guilty, which his own conscience knows, the Lord give him repentance for this so inhuman and barbarous fact, or else undoubtedly the just God will in due time avenge this innocent blood. This fact, when heard of, was deservedly abhorred by all sober persons. Those poor Christian Indians of Wamesit escaped clear away, and joined themselves with Wannalencet, who had withdrawn himself in the beginning of the war. They suffered much in their peregrination (as we afterward understood), and sundry of them died by sickness, whereof two were principal (and I hope pious) men ; the one named Numphow, their chief ruler, and the other Mystic George, a teacher of them ; besides divers other men, women, and children, through famine and sickness lost their lives. The rest of them, in August following, came in with Wannalancet to Major Walderne, and the rest of the committee at Cocheco, who were appointed to treat and make peace with such as came in and surrendered ; these Wamesitt Indians, as well as Wannalancet and his people, had not been in hostility against the English, nor had done them any wrong, only fled away for fear, and for wrongs suffered from some English ; so that there lay no just block in the way unto their reconciliation, so they were accepted ; and yet, afterward, when they were sent to Boston, accusations came against some of them by English captives escaped, that some of them were in arms against the English, (how true those charges were God only knows, for 't is very difficult, unless upon long knowledge, to distinguish Indians from one another,) however, the testimony of the witnesses against them were admitted, and some of them condemned to death and executed, and others sent to Islands out of the country ; but some few were pardoned and reconciled, whereof Wannalancet and six or seven of his men were a part, and the Wamesit Indians, Sam Numphow (hardly escaped), Symon Betokam, Jonathan, George, a brother to Sam Numphow, and very few other men, but several women and children, who now lived among the rest.

1675. Upon the 21st day of February, the General Court

of Massachusetts convened, according to a former adjournment. As soon as they were met, tidings were brought them,
that a body of the enemy, about four hundred, had attacked
that morning a town called Medfield, about eighteen miles from
Boston west southerly, (and although it be a digression yet I
shall take liberty to give a particular account of it, because
occasion was taken hereby to bring more trouble and affliction
upon the Christian Indians ; and also it may serve, once for all,
for an example of the manner and methods of the enemies'
proceeding against the English in this war ; and give you a
taste of their pride and insolence, and the craft and subtlety
used by them in their enterprises, especially at this time when
they were in their highest raffe.)

Upon the 21st day of February, 1675, very early in the
morning, a considerable body of Indians, between three and
four hundred, in the preceding night (or rather a little before
day), conveyed themselves secretly into every part of the
town,* especially in the south-east end, next Dedham, having
fitted themselves with combustible matter, and therewith set
several houses on fire, as it were in one instant of time, planting
men in ambushment near the houses, that as soon as the
people came forth they might shoot them down, as they did.
There was at this time in the town a foot company of soldiers,
under command of Capt. Jacob, of about eighty men, and a
ply of horse under command of Cornet Oakes, about twenty,
and of the trained band of the town about one hundred men,
the whole about two hundred well armed ; but they being
quartered scatteringly in the town, (excepting about thirty men
that were upon the watch at the *corps du garde*, near the
meeting-house,) in which respect they could not get together
into a body to repel the enemy, until they were withdrawn
and retreated out of the town ; for, as soon as the alarm was
taken, those at the main guard firing a great gun three or
four times over, gave the alarm effectually, insomuch that the
Indians saw cause to withdraw on a bridge towards Sherburne,
and firing the bridge impeded the pursuit of the English
soldiers. The enemy drew up in a body on the other side of
the river, and, being secure, vapored and talked high. But
the English soldiers could not get to them, because the bridge
was cut off ; as is before mentioned. Before the enemy retreated they burnt about forty dwelling-houses, which was near

---

* Medfield.

half the town, and slew and wounded about twenty persons, whereof the lieutenant of the town, named Adams, (a person somewhat severe against the praying Indians) was one ; and the same night the lieutenant's widow, being at Mr. Wilson's, the minister's house, that stood near the main guard, being upon a bed in a chamber, divers soldiers and commanders being in the room underneath, Capt. Jacob having a gun in his hand half bent, with the muzzle upward towards the chamber, he being taking his leave to be gone to his quarters, by some accident the gun fired through, and shot floor, mat, and through and through the body of the lieutenant's widow, that lay upon the bed, and slew her also; this was a very strange accident, but God is awful in such tremendous dispensations. This intelligence of burning Medfield coming to the General Court, and so soon after the burning of Lancaster, occasioned many thoughts of hearty and hurrying motions, and gave opportunity to the vulgar to cry out, "Oh, come, let us go down to Deer Island, and kill all the praying Indians." They could not come at the enemy Indians, for they were too crafty and subtle for the English ; therefore they would have wreaked their rage upon the poor unarmed Indians our friends, (had not the authority of the country restrained them ;) for about this time the Council was informed by good testimony, that about thirty or forty men were entering into a combination, to convey themselves out to the Island, at Pulling Point, the narrowest place between it and the main, and to have cut off all the poor Christain Indians.   But the Council sent for two or three of the persons, and warned them, at their peril, to desist from such a wicked action ; and so the project was frustrated.

There was a paper written by the enemy Indians, and stuck up in a cleft of one of the bridge posts at Medfield, which being found by an English trooper belonging to Captain Gibbs,* who brought it to his Captain, the contents whereof were ;

"Know by this paper, that the Indians that thou hast provoked to wrath and anger, will war this twenty one years if you will ; there are many Indians yet, we come three hundred at this time. You must consider the Indians lost nothing but their life ; you must lose your fair houses and cattle."

This paper was brought to the General Court, wherein may be seen the pride and insolence of these barbarians at this

----

* Captain Benjamin Gibbs.

time. But the great God and our only Saviour hath for his name's sake rebuked their rage, and broken them in pieces like a potter's vessel. To God be all the glory.

About this time, there befell another great trouble and exercise to the Christian Indians of Nashobah, who sojourned in Concord by order; the matter was this. The Council had, by several orders, empowered a committee, who, with the consent of the selectmen of Concord, settled those Indians at that town, under the government and tuition of Mr. John Hoare; the number of those Indians were about fifty-eight of all sorts, whereof were not above twelve able men, the rest were women and children. These Indians lived very soberly, and quietly, and industriously, and were all unarmed; neither could any of them be charged with any unfaithfulness to the English interest. In pursuance of this settlement, Mr. Hoare had begun to build a large and convenient work-house for the Indians, near his own dwelling; which stood about the midst of the town, and very nigh the town watch-house. This house was made, not only to secure those Indians under lock and key by night, but to employ them and set them to work by day, whereby they earned their own bread, and in an ordinary way (with God's blessing) would have lived well in a short time. But some of the inhabitants of the town, being influenced with a spirit of animosity and distaste against all Indians, disrelished this settlement; and therefore privately sent to a Captain of the army,* that quartered his company not far off at that time, of whom they had experience, that he would not be backward to put in execution any thing that tended to distress the praying Indians; for this was the same man that had formerly, without order, seized upon divers of the praying Indians at Marlborough, which brought much trouble and disquiet to the country of the Indians, and was a great occasion of their defection; as hath been above declared. This Captain accordingly came to Concord with a party of his men, upon the Sabbath day, into the meeting-house, where the people were convened in the worship of God. And after the exercise was ended, he spake openly to the congregation to this effect: "That he understood there were some heathen in the town, committed to one Hoare, which he was informed were a trouble and disquiet to them; therefore if they desired it, he would remove them to Boston;" to which speech of his, most

---

* Captain Mosely.

of the people being silent, except two or three that encouraged
him, he took, as it seems, the silence of the rest for consent;
and immediately after the assembly were dismissed, he went
with three or four files of men, and a hundred or two of the
people, men, women, and children, at his heels, and marched
away to Mr. Hoare's house, and there demanded of him to
see the Indians under his care. Hoare opened the door and
showed them to him, and they were all numbered and found
there; the Captain then said to Mr. Hoare, that he would
leave a corporal and soldiers to secure them; but Mr. Hoare
answered, there was no need of that, for they were already
secured, and were committed to him by order of the Council,
and he would keep and secure them. But yet the Captain left
his corporal and soldiers there, who were abusive enough to
the poor Indians by ill language. The next morning the
Captain came again, to take the Indians and send them to
Boston. But Mr. Hoare refused to deliver them unless he
showed him an order of the Council; but the Captain could
show him no other but his commission to kill and destroy
the enemy; but Mr. Hoare said, these were friends and under
order. But the Captain would not be satisfied with his answer,
but commanded his corporal forthwith to break open the door
and take the Indians all away, which was done accordingly;
and some of the soldiers plundered the poor creatures of their
shirts, shoes, dishes, and such other things as they could lay
their hands upon, though the Captain commanded the contrary.
They were all brought to Charlestown with a guard of twenty
men. And the Captain wrote a letter to the General Court,
then sitting, giving them an account of his action. This thing
was very offensive to the Council, that a private captain
should (without commission or some express order) do an
act so contradictory to their former orders; and the Governor
and several others spake of it at a conference with the Deputies at the General Court, manifesting their dissatisfaction
at this great irregularity, in setting up a military power in
opposition to the chief authority of the country; declaring of
what evil consequence such a precedent was; instancing the ill
effects of the like practices in England in latter times; urging
that due testimony might be borne against the same, by the
whole Court. The Deputies seemed generally to agree to the
reason of the magistrates in this matter; yet, notwithstanding,
the Captain (who appeared in the Court shortly after, upon

another occasion,) met with no rebuke for this high irregularity and arbitrary action. To conclude this matter, those poor Indians about fifty-eight of them of all sorts, were sent down to Deer Island, there to pass into the furnace of affliction with their brethren and countrymen. But all their corn and other provision, sufficient to maintain them for six months, was lost at Concord; and all their other necessaries, except what the soldiers had plundered. And the poor Indians got very little or nothing of what they lost, but it was squandered away, lost by the removal of Mr. Hoare and other means, so that they were necessitated to live upon clams as the others did, with some little corn provided at the charge of the Honorable Corporation for the Indians, residing in London. Besides, Mr. Hoare lost all his building, and other cost, which he had provided for the entertainment and employment of those Indians; which was considerable.

1675, Feb'y 23d. About this time (the General Court then sitting), there were several motions and applications made to them touching the poor Christian Indians at Deer Island. Some would have them all destroyed; others, sent out of the country; but some there were of more moderation, alleging that those Indians and their ancestors had a covenant with the English about thirty years since, wherein mutual protection and subjection was agreed; and that it was expedient to search the records to see and consider that agreement, and whether those Indians had broken the same, or had deserved to be proceeded against in so harsh and severe a manner as some proposed; upon which motion the records were searched, and it was found upon record, as follows.

" At a General Court held at Boston in New England, the 7th of the first month, 164¾.

Magistrates Present.

John Winthrop, Esq'r., Gov'r.,	Simon Bradstreet, Esq'r.,
John Endicot, Dept. Gov'r.,	William Hibins, Esq'r.,
Thomas Dudley, Esq'r.,	Thomas Flint, Esq'r.,
Richard Bolingham,	Samuel Symonds, Esq'r.,
John Winthrop, Jun'r., Esq'r.,	Increase Nowell, Esq'r., Sec.

Deputies Present.

Mr. William Hilton,	Mr. Lowell,
Mr. Howard,	Mr. Henry Short,
Mr. Samuel Dudley,	Mr. Matthew Boyse,
Mr. Winsley,	Mr. Edward Carleton,

Mr. Daniel Denison,
Mr. John Tuttle,
Mr. Joseph Bachelor,
Mr. Nicholas Norton,
Mr. Emanuel Downing,
Mr. William Hathorne,
Mr. Robert Bridges,
Mr. Edward Tomlins,
Mr. Robert Sedgwick,
Mr. Edward Sprague,
Mr. George Cook,
Mr. Samuel Shepard,
Mr. Mahue,
Mr. Mason,
Mr. Lusher,
Mr. Chickering,

Mr. Willard,
Mr. Hayne,
Mr. Hawkins,
Mr. Tyng,
Mr. Weld,
Mr. Johnson,
Mr. Glover,
Mr. Duncan,
Mr. Casse,
Mr. Peter Bracket,
Mr. Torrey,
Mr. Hollister,
Mr. Ames,
Mr. Joshua Hubard,
Mr. Stephen Winthrop.

"Wassamequin,* Nashoonon, Kutchamaquin, Massaconomet, and Squaw Sachem, did voluntarily submit themselves to us; as appears by their covenant subscribed with their own hands here following, and other articles to which they consented.

"We have, and by these presents, do, voluntarily and without any constraint or persuasion, but of our own free motion, put ourselves, our subjects, our lands and estates, under the government and jurisdiction of Massachusetts; to be governed and protected by them, according to their just laws and orders, so far as we shall be made capable of understanding them; and we do promise, for ourselves and all our subjects and all our posterity, to be true and faithful to the said government, and aiding to the maintenance thereof, to our best ability. And from time to time to give speedy notice of any conspiracy, attempt, or cruel intention of any that we shall know or hear of against the same. And we do promise to be willing from time to time to be instructed in the knowledge of God. In witness whereof, we have hereunto put our hands, the eighth day of the first month, 164$\frac{3}{4}$.

" MASSANOMIT,
KUTSHAMAQUIN,
SQUAW SACHEM,
NASHOONON,
WASSAMEQUIN.

* For an account of this, and most of the other chiefs here named, see *Book of the Indians*.

"*Certain Questions propounded to the Indians, and their Answers.*

"*Q.* 1. To worship the only true God, who made heaven and earth.

"*Ans.* We do desire to reverence the God of the English, because we see he doth better to the English than other gods do to others.

"*Q.* 2. Not to swear falsely.

"*Ans.* They say they know not what swearing is among them.

"*Q.* 3. Not to do any unnecessary work on the Sabbath day, especially within the gates of Christian towns.

"*Ans.* It is easy to them; they have not much to do on any day, and they can well take their rest on that day.

"*Q.* 4. To honor their parents and superiors.

"*Ans.* 'T is their custom to do so, for the inferiors to honor their superiors.

"*Q.* 5. To kill no man without just cause and just authority.

"*Ans.* This is good, and they desire to do so.

"*Q.* 6. To commit no unclean lust, as for instance, adultery, incest, rape, sodomy, bigamy, or beastiality.

"*Ans.* Though sometimes some of them do it, yet they account it naught.

"*Q.* 7. Not to steal.

"*Ans.* They said to this as to the 6th *quere.*

"*Q.* 8. To suffer their children to learn to read God's word, that they may learn to know God aright, and to worship him in his own way.

"*Ans.* They say, as opportunity will serve, and the English live among them, they desire so to do.

"*Q.* 9. That they should not be idle.

"*Ans.* To which and all the rest they consented, acknowledging them to be good.

"Being received by us, they presented twenty six fathom of wampum. And the Court directed the treasurer to give them four coats, two yards in a coat, of red cloth, and a potful of wine.*

* The following is the entry made by Governor Winthrop in his Journal, relating to this matter. "At this Court, Cutshamekin and Squaw Sachem, Masconomo, Nashacowan and Wassamagoin, two Sachems near the great hill to the west, called Wachusett, came into the

" This above is a true copy taken out of the record of the
General Court, Book 2, page 64 ; as attests
EDWARD RAWSON, *Secretary.*"

The praying Indians, confined to Deer Island, are the people
with whom the above written agreements were made, wherein
subjection and mutual protection are engaged ; and these Indians, as is before declared, made discovery of what they knew
of the plottings and conspiracy of the enemy, before the war
began ; also most readily and cheerfully joined with, and assisted
the English in the war ; as is before in part touched, and will
more clearly appear in the sequel of this discourse ; also they
submitted themselves to the laws of God and the English
government, and desiring themselves and children to be
taught and instructed in the Christian religion ; and have in all
other points, so far as I know, (for the body of them,) kept and
performed the articles of their covenant above expressed. When
the General Court had read and considered this agreement, it
had this effect (through God's grace) in some degree to abate
the clamors of many men against these Indians.

1675.   Before the General Court adjourned, which was not
until the 28th of February, they had voted and concluded to
raise an army of six hundred men, to be put under the conduct
of Major Thomas Savage,* as Commander-in-chief ; but the
Major was not willing to undertake the charge, unless he might
have some of the Christian Indians upon Deer Island to go
with him for guides, &c. ; for the Major, being an experienced
soldier, well considered the great necessity of such helps in
such an undertaking. The General Court consented to this reasonable motion of Major Savage, and accordingly ordered that
one John Curtis, of Roxbury, (who was well acquainted with
those Indians,) should go down to Deer Island and choose out

Court, and, according to their former tender to the governor, desired to
be received under our protection and government, upon the same terms
that Pumham and Socononoco were ; so, we causing them to understand
the articles and all the ten commandments of God, and they freely
assenting to all, they were solemnly received, and then presented the
Court with twenty six fathom more of wampom ; and the Court gave
each of them a coat of two yd's. of cloth, and their dinner ; and to
them and their men, every of them, a cup of sack at their departure ; so
they took leave and went away."— *History of New England,* II. 156.
  * For an account of this good officer and gentleman, see Farmer's
Register, and Mr. James Savage's *Notes to Winthrop's Journal.*

six of the fittest men for that service, which he did, and chose and brought up with him six men, whose names were James Quannapohit, Job Kattenanit, (those were the two spies before mentioned,) James Speen, Andrew Pitimee, John Magus, and William Nahaton. These were all principal men, faithful and courageous; they were all willing, and cheerful, and joyful, that they had this call and opportunity to serve the English under Major Savage, whom some of them had served under, in the beginning of the war at Mount Hope. These six men, being fitted and furnished with arms and other necessaries, they were conducted to Marlborough, from whence the army was to march the first day of March, 167$\frac{5}{6}$.

But before the army set forth from Marlborough, there fell out a matter of trouble and disquiet to them, occasioned by the motion of one of the captains* of the army, of whom it hath been once and again declared that he was no lover of the praying Indians; and because the matter referreth to one of the six Indians before named, now with the army, it seems pertinent to my purpose to declare it. Job Kattenanit, when he returned from the service he had done as one of the spies, obtained leave from the Council to endeavour to fulfil an agreement he had made with some of the Christian Indians, among the enemy, particularly with Joseph Tuckapawilin, minister of the Indian Church, late at Hassanamesit, and others, to meet them in the woods about those parts, and bring with them Job's three children again to the English. In pursuance of this order of the Council, Major Savage did (with the advice and consent of Major-General Dennison, who was then at Marlborough in order to despatch away the army) give liberty to Job to go alone from Marlborough to the place appointed, about Hassanamesit, not above twelve miles distant, to meet his friends and children, and to bring them in to the army at the rendezvous at Quabage. Not long after Job was gone from Marlboro', the captain aforesaid, hearing of it, made a very great stir at the head-quarters at William Ward's, in Marlborough, where the army was drawn up in a body in order to their march; and spake words reflecting greatly upon that action of sending away Job, alleging that he would inform the enemy of the army's motion, and so frustrate the whole design. This fair pretence was managed in a mutinous manner by others of like temper and spirit, insomuch that the army was under great disquiet; hereby the wisdom and prudence not only

* Mosely.

of Major Savage, but of Major-General Denson, was much reflected upon. But they were fain to calm this storm by gentle means and soft words, and forthwith ordered to send away Capt. Wadsworth and Capt. Syll, who offered themselves, with James Quannapohit, to follow Job on horseback, hoping to overtake him and prevent that which was feared. Accordingly they were speedily despatched to pursue Job; which had a tendency to compose and qualify the heats that were begotten upon this occasion. But Wadsworth and Syll did not overtake Job nor meet him till he was returned to the army; nor yet did Job meet with his friends, but found signs where they had lately been; for those poor creatures had shifted their quarters for fear, because the time was expired that Job promised to meet them, if he were admitted. But Job, missing his friends, faithfully fulfilled his promise in returning to the army, whom he met upon the road about twenty miles westward of Marlborough; and so proved himself an honest man, and that those suspicions of him were groundless. I conceive, had this mutinous practice (that so much reflected upon the chief commander of the army and authority of the Council) been committed in some other parts of the world, it would have cost the author of it a cashiering at least, if not a more severe animadversion; for it was an action against the order and good discipline of an army, for any private captain to animadvert (in such a manner) upon the general's actions, done with consideration and prudence. Those poor Christian Indians before mentioned, (with Job's children,) although Job could not meet them, yet were met by Capt. Benjamin Gibbs and a small party of horse under his command, who, scouting in the woods as the army were upon their march to Quabage, took those poor creatures (supposing they had got a prize); they were but two men (one very aged),* three women, and six children. The soldiers that seized them took from them all those few necessaries they had preserved; as two rugs, two brass kettles, some dishes, and a pewter cup, that the minister † had saved, which he was wont to use at the administration of the sacrament of the Lord's Supper, being given him by Mr. Elliot for their use; in a word, the soldiers took all the little they had, and told many stories concerning them, that so they might not return their things again. But yet God so ordered it, that they hurt not their bodies, but brought them in to the General Savage, at the rendezvous, who understanding they were Job's

---

* Naoas.   † Tuckapawillin, son of Naoas.

friends and his children, he treated them civilly, and forthwith
sent them with a guard back to Marlborough, to be conveyed to
Boston. But when the poor creatures came to Marlborough,
they being quartered there one night or two by the constable's
order, until an opportunity served to send them on to Boston,
there came some people of the town (especially women) to their
quarter, some of whom did so abuse, threaten, and taunt at these
poor Christians, and they being thereby put into great fears, that
in the night the minister's * wife, and his eldest son, a lad of
twelve years old, and another woman, a widow that had carefully
kept and nourished Job's children, with her daughter, being four
of them in all, escaped away into the woods; the minister's wife
left a nursing infant behind her, with her husband, of about
three months old, which affliction was a very sore trial to the
poor man, his wife and eldest son gone, and the poor infant
no breast to nourish it. I heard a prudent gentleman, one
Capt. Brattle of Boston, who was then at Marlborough, (for he
heard the people's taunts and threats to them,) say, that he was
ashamed to see and hear what he did of that kind, and, if he
had been an Indian and so abused, he should have run away as
they did. Not long after, this poor minister, Joseph Tuckappawillin, and his aged father, Naaos, a man of about eighty years
old, both good Christians, with three or four children of the
minister's, and Job's three children, were all sent to Boston,
where they were kept a night or two, and then sent to Deer
Island, where God provided a nurse (among the Indians) to
preserve the life of the sucking infant; and about two months
after, his wife was recovered and brought in by Tom Dublet,†
one of our messengers to the enemy; but his eldest son before
mentioned died, after he went away from Marlborough with his
mother, conceived to lose his life by famine. The other widow,
who went away at that time, and her daughter, were also recovered. This widow Job married afterward, not knowing how
better to requite her love showed in nourishing and preferring
his three children when they were among the enemies, and
they now lived comfortably together; so that after all the troubles, sorrows, and calamities this man Job underwent, (as we
have before touched,) God gave him all his children in safety,

---

* Tuckapawillin.

† He was very successful in negotiating with the Nipmuks. In *The
Book of the Indians* is given his biography, under the name of Nepa-
net.

and a suitable wife; and vindicated him from all the calumnies and aspersions cast on him, and by good demonstrations cleared his integrity and faithfulness to God's cause and the English interest, and hath made him very serviceable and victorious since, in the war against the enemy.

One thing I shall further mention, that is of remark, before I pass the history of the matter. Joseph Tuckapawillin, minister and pastor of the church at Hassanamesit before spoken of, while he was at Boston, and before he was sent to Deer Island, some persons had compassion on his distressed condition, particularly Capt. Nicholas Page and his wife, who took him, and his children, and his aged father, to their house in Boston, and refreshed their bowels with food and other comforts, and milk to preserve the poor infant's life. This poor man was much affected with, and thankful for their love. While he was at Capt. Page's, Mr. John Elliot (his spiritual father in Christ) came to visit him, with some others formerly acquainted with him, and spake divers words of comfort to him, suitable to his condition; divers things were spoken to him and wisely answered by him, which I shall not mention, but one passage I noted, being present. Said Joseph to Mr. Elliot, "Oh, Sir," said he, "I am greatly distressed this day on every side; the English have taken away some of my estate, my corn, cattle, my plough, cart, chain, and other goods. The enemy Indians have also taken a part of what I had; and the wicked Indians mock and scoff at me, saying, ' Now what is become of your praying to God?' The English also censure me, and say I am a hypocrite. In this distress I have no where to look, but up to God in heaven to help me; now my dear wife and eldest son are (through the English threatenings) run away, and I fear will perish in the woods for want of food; also my aged mother is lost; and all this doth greatly aggravate my grief. But yet I desire to look up to God in Christ Jesus, in whom alone is my help." Being asked by Capt. Page, whether he had not assisted the enemy in the wars when he was among them; he answered, " I never did join with them against the English. Indeed, they often solicited me, but I utterly denied and refused it. I thought within myself, it is better to die than to fight against the church of Christ." I questioned him many things of the condition and number of the enemy; he answered, that he judged they were about a thousand men; " but," said he, " the greatest part, as I conceive, are for peace, and not to hold on the war; and," said he, " shortly they will be in great straits for food, when the ground-nuts are gone."

Now we come in order to declare something concerning the six Indians that went with Major Savage, to find out the enemy at Menumesse. There wanted not some who, in their letters from the army, accused Job of false dealing, and that he had informed the enemy of our army's coming against them. But neither the general (Major Savage), nor Mr. Nowel, the minister of the army, intimated any such matter in their letters to the Council, but rather the contrary; and, because I was not present with them to observe the actings of those Indians, I shall content myself with writing the extract of Mr. Nowell's letter, concerning the carriage and deportment of those six Indians. This gentleman was the principal minister of the army, a pious and prudent person, and is minister of God's word at Boston, in New England. His letter was dated March 26th, 1676; wherein, after salutations and giving a particular account of the motions of the army, from the time they went forth until that day, saith he, " I look at it as a great rebuke of God, that we should miss our enemy as we did, when we were at Menumesse. If we had hearkened to those six Indians whom we took from Deer Island, we might have prevented that error. They have behaved themselves like sober, honest men, since their abode with us, which hath made me look after them more carefully. At their first coming to Hadley, the man with whom they quartered allowed them pork and peas enough, but not bread; he perceiving they had some money, made them buy their bread. When they had laid out about 4s 6d., one of them told me of it; upon which I spake to the gentlemen, who ordered the constable to allow them bread, and I did them give 4s. 6d. out of my own purse, to reimburse what they had expended. And, whereas some have accused Job for discovering to the Indians our coming forth with the army, I could easily demonstrate that it was not possible for him to go to Menumesse to make any such discovery, while he was absent from Marlborough. But the circumstances of that story are so many, it would be too long to commit them to writing at present. I question not Job's uprightness towards the English, and shall make it out, if the Lord bring me back." He further adds, in the same letter, that the Natick Indians took two of the enemy, which being sullen were slain, and of their advice for pursuing the enemy, which was not attended, and so the opportunity was frustrated; and several other passages he relates of them, declaring their prudence, and fidelity, and courage. Again, in another letter from the same person, dated April 9th, which was about the time of the army's return home as far as Marlborough, saith he, "Our pilots (*i. e.* the Indians) were labored with to represent the way to watch [Watchuset?] (where the body of the enemy quartered) very difficult, before they came to speak before the Council; and had ill words given them, that so they might be afraid to speak any thing that should afford encouragement. The poor Indians, our pilots, as soon as they arrived at Marlborough, were much abused by the townsmen, insomuch that they were unwilling to go into any house." Thus much of Mr. Nowell's letters, touching those six Indians, of whom the general also gave a good character.

167⅘. In the months of February, March, and April, the enemy Indians were very violent in their attempts and assaults upon all the frontier English plantations, burning several villages * or part of them, and murdering many people in the highways; † so that weekly, yea almost daily, messengers with sad tidings were brought into the Council, insomuch that the Lord seemed to threaten great calamity to ensue upon the English nation; for none of our enterprises against the enemy were blessed with success, and it was groundedly feared and judged that seed-time and harvest would be greatly obstructed, and thereby occasion famine to follow the war. These things occasion great thoughts of heart unto the godly wise, especially such as were at the helm of government; and the rather because God seemed to put us to shame, and not to go forth with our arms, but to render our endeavours to quell the rage and fury of the enemy fruit-less. In this conjunction of our affairs, some made application to the Council, to arm and send forth a company of the Christian Indians that were at Deer Island, who had manifested themselves very desirous and willing to engage against the enemy in this distressing time; particularly Capt. Daniel Hench-man, who was appointed by the Council to look to the Indians at Deer Island, and to put them upon employ. This gentle-

---

* Warwick, Lancaster, Medfield, Weymouth, Groton, Marlborough, Rehoboth, Providence, and many other places were among those destroyed or damaged.

† "May 3, at Haverhill and Bradford, a small company of Indians killed two men, and carried away a man and woman and five children captive." — *I. Mather*, 28.

man made motions to the Council, once and again, of his readiness to conduct these Indians against the enemy; declaring that
he had great confidence in God, that if they were employed
they might, with God's blessing, be instrumental to give check
to the enemy and turn the alarm; testifying that he found them
very willing and desirous to serve the country, and leave their
parents, wives, and children under the English power, which
would be rational security to the English for their fidelity. But
those motions were not accepted at first; for God's time was not
yet come for our deliverance, and the Indian rod had not yet
smarted sufficiently. The people generally distrusted those
praying Indians, and were not willing to have any of them employed to serve the country; which was the principal reason
why the Council complied not with those and former motions
of this nature, for many of the Council were otherwise opposed
enough to it. Indeed afterwards the motion to arm and employ the Christian Indians, was embraced and put in practice;
of which we shall speak in its proper place. But some other
matters previous to it were first done, which I shall now relate.

Mr. Rowlandson, minister of Lancaster, (a pious and good
man,) having his wife, children, and several friends in captivity
among the enemy, being surprised at Lancaster as is before
touched; himself, and several other ministers in his behalf, had
some time since petitioned the Council to use what means they
could for the redemption of his wife, &c.; which the Council
consented to, and, in pursuance thereof, ordered Major Gookin
to endeavour to procure at Deer Island one or two Indians, that
for a reward might adventure to go with a message to the
enemy, to offer for the redemption of our captives, particularly
Mrs. Rowlandson. But, although the Major went to the Island,
and did his utmost endeavours to procure an Indian to adventure
upon this service at that time, yet could not prevail with any;
so the matter lay dormant a good space of time.

But, on the 23d of March, some friends advised Mr. Rowlandson to make another petition to revive the former motion;
which he did that day. The Council declared themselves
ready to promote it, and send a messenger, if any could be procured. Major Gookin, who stirred up Mr. Rowlandson hereunto, was informed that one of the Indians lately brought down
from Concord, named Tom Dublot, *alias* Nepponit, had some
inclination to run that adventure; of which the Major informing
the Council, they ordered Capt. Henchman to treat and agree

with him, which he accordingly did, and brought him up from
Deer Island some few days after; and he was sent to Major
Gookin's, at Cambridge, where he was, according to the order
of the Council, fitted and furnished for this enterprise; and had
a letter from the Council to the enemy, concerning the redemption of the captives; and upon Monday, April 3d, he was sent
away from Cambridge upon his journey; and he did effect it
with care and prudence, and returned again upon the 12th of
April, with this answer in writing, from the enemy: —

"To Governor and Council in Boston, and people that are
in war with us.

"We now give answer by this one man; but if you like my
answer, send one more man besides this Tom Neppanit, and
send with all true heart, and with all your mind, by two men.
Because you know, and we know, you have great sorrowful
with crying; for you lost many, many hundred men, and all
your house, all your land, and woman, child, and cattle, and
all your things that you have lost." Moreover they add, that
Mrs. Rowlandson and other captives are alive. This was signed by Sam and Kutquen Quanohit, sagamores, and Peter Jethro, scribe. To this letter the Council gave answer, tending to
abate their pride and insolence; and sent again Tom Neppanit,
and another Indian named Peter Conway, to move further
about the redemption of Mrs. Rowlandson and her friends,
which the enemy inclined unto. Those two Indians were
sent a second, third, and fourth time, and some English with
them; and at last prevailed so far, that Mrs. Rowlandson and
some others were redeemed, and brought home about the
Election time following. This treaty about the captives, and
the consequences thereof, had no small influence into the
abatement of the enemy's violence and our troubles, and had
a tendency to dividing them and break their union, and consequently their strength; for Philip, and some others of the
enemy's chief men, were utterly against treating with the
English or surrendering the captives. But some other of
their principal sachems, that were more inclinable to a reconciliation with the English, thought that their compliance with
the English about surrendering the captives (especially being
well paid for their redemption) would mollify the Englishmen's
minds in order to a peace. This contest about the treaty,
caused them to fall out and divide. Philip and most of the

Narraganset Indians separated from the inland Indians, and went down into their own country, and the inland Indians staid about Wachuset mountain; which was a means under God to weaken and destroy them, as might be showed, and is in part declared already, in the history of the war published. This was another piece of service done by our praying Indians; at least they broke the ice and made way for it, by their first adventuring to treat with the enemy. Whilst this matter of the redemption of the captives was in agitation, the assaults of the enemy were frequent and violent, for the body of them quartered within twenty miles of the English frontiers of Lancaster, Groton, and Marlborough, and made daily incursions upon us; and notwithstanding the Council had used many endeavours, and raised forces and sent them forth, to beat up their head quarters at Watchusett, all those means proved ineffectual; and the enemy still kept that station, the place being near a very high mountain, and very difficult to have access to, by reason of thick woods and rocks and other fastnesses, that our English army thought it not advisable to hazard themselves in that enterprise. In this juncture of affairs, the Council at last resolved to arm and send forth a company of the praying Indians from Deer Island, under the conduct of Samuel Hunting and James Richardson, the one made a captain, the other his lieutenant, for this service; these two Englishmen were well acquainted with those Indians, and persons whom they told. In pursuance whereof Capt. Hunting had orders and a commission, and did his best endeavour; but could not (at that time) procure arms for more than forty Indians. Indeed, those praying Indians had generally arms of their own before the war began; but they were taken away from them by the English, and squandered away many of them, as at Marlborough twenty-seven good arms at one time, before touched; and some taken by Sudbury men at the falls on Charles River, and detained to this day, and others from particular persons; those were all taken from them without order, and upward of twenty arms were taken from them after they were confined to the Island; those last were part of the arms wherewith they were now furnished.

Upon the 21st of April, Capt. Hunting had drawn up and ready furnished his company of forty Indians, at Charlestown. They were ordered by the Council at first to march up to Merrimack river near Chelmsford, and there to settle a garrison near the great fishing-places, where it was expected the enemy would come at this season to get fish for their necessary food; and from this fort to keep their scouts abroad daily, to seize the enemy; and if they should be overpowered by greater numbers, their garrison and fort was for their retreat, until assistance might be sent them. This was the projection of this undertaking at first; and accordingly matters were prepared, and carriages with provisions and tools sent away to Merrimack river. But behold God's thoughts are not as ours, nor his ways as ours: for just as those Indian soldiers were ready to march, upon the 21st of April, about mid-day tidings came by many messengers, that a great body of the enemy, not less as was judged than fifteen hundred; (for the enemy, to make their force seem to be very great, there were many women among them, whom they had fitted with pieces of wood cut in the form of guns, which those carried, and were placed in the centre;) they had assaulted a town called Sudbury, that morning, and set fire of sundry houses and barns of that town, (this town is about eighteen miles from Charlestown, westerly;) giving an account that the people of the place were greatly distressed and earnestly desired succor; indeed (thro' God's favor) some small assistance was already sent from Watertown, by Capt. Hugh Mason,* which was the next town to Sudbury. These with some of the inhabitants joined, and with some others that came in to their help, there was vigorous resistance made, and a check given to the enemy, so that those that were gotten over the river, to the east side of the town, were forced to retreat; and the body of the enemy were repulsed that they could not pass the bridge, which pass the English kept. But those particulars were not known when the tidings came to Charlestown, where the Indian companies before mentioned were ready. Just at the beginning of the Lecture there, as soon as these tidings came, Major Gookin and Mr. Thomas Danforth, (two of the magistrates,) who were then hearing the Lecture Sermon, being acquainted herewith, withdrew out of the meeting-house, and immediately gave orders for a ply of horse, belonging to Capt. Prentiss' troops, under conduct of Corporal Phipps, and the Indian company under Capt. Hunting, forthwith to march away

---

* He was of Watertown; freeman, 1635; representative in the General Court for ten years; died, 1678.

for the relief of Sudbury; which accordingly was put in execution.   Capt. Hunting with his Indian company, being on foot, got not to Sudbury until a little within night.

The enemy, as is before touched, were all retreated unto the west side of the river of Sudbury, where also several English inhabited.   Upon the 22d of April, early in the morning, our forty Indians, having stripped themselves, and painted their faces like to the enemy, they passed over the bridge to the west side of the river, without any Englishmen in their company, to make discovery of the enemy, (which was generally conceived quartered thereabout.)   But this did not at all discourage our Christian Indians from marching out for discovery, and if they had met with them, to beat up their quarters.   But God had so ordered it, that the enemy were all withdrawn and were retreated in the night.   Our Indian soldiers, having made a thorough discovery, and to their great grief, (for some of them wept when they saw so many English lie dead on the place among the slain;) some they knew, viz. those two worthy and pious captains, Capt. Brocklebank of Rowley, and Capt. Wadsworth * of Milton, who, with about thirty-two private soldiers, were slain the day before.   For Capt. Wadsworth, lying with his company at Marlborough, being left there to strengthen that frontier, upon the return of the army; he, understanding that the enemy had attacked Sudbury, took a ply of his men, about six files, and marched for their relief, with whom Capt. Brocklebank (who kept quarters at Marlborough) went, taking this opportunity, as a good convoy, to go to Boston to speak with the Council. Capt. Wadsworth, being a valiant and active man, and being very desirous to rescue his friends at Sudbury, marched in the night with all the speed he could; and his soldiers, being spent and weary with travel and want of rest, fell into the enemy's ambushment in the morning; and the enemy, being numerous, encompassed him round, so that they were generally cut off, except a few that escaped to a mill which was fortified, but the people were fled out of it; but the enemy knew not of their flight, and so, supposing the mill to be strong, they ventured not to attack it.   At the same time, Capt. Cutler of Charlestown, with a small company,† having the convoy of

---

* The monument which now marks the place of this fight, was erected by a son of Capt. Wadsworth, who was President of Harvard College.
† Consisting of *eleven*, according to Mr. Hubbard.

some carts from Marlborough, that were coming to Sudbury, having secured his carriage at a garrison-house, escaped narrowly from being cut off by the enemy. The enemy also, at that time, cut off some English soldiers that were coming down under the conduct of one Cowell, of Boston, that had been a convoy to some provisions at Quabage fort.* But I have too far digressed. Therefore, to return to the company of our Christian Indians, who, as soon as they had made a full discovery, returned to their captain and the rest of the English, and gave them an account of their motions. Then it was concluded to march over to the place and bury the dead, and they did so shortly, after, that day, our Indians marching in two files upon the wings, to secure those that went to bury the dead. God so ordered it, that they met with no interruption in that work. Our Indians found only four dead Indians of the enemy, covered up with logs and rubbish. This service, so faithfully performed by our Christian Indians, had the effect to abate much, with many, their former hatred of them, especially at Sudbury, some of the people who had formerly done much injury to these our Christian friends, whilst they dwelt at Natick, for some of them know they have taken several things from them, and never restored them; as guns, utensils for carts and ploughs, corn and swine, and materials of ironwork belonging to a sawmill, and other things; their consciences can best witness what they are; and if they do not make restitution, I fear they will have little comfort at death, though they please themselves with this notion, that the enemy Indians robbed and plundered them of such like things; but this will not be (I contend) a sufficient warrant to wrong the innocent, or rob honest men, because thieves of the same nation have robbed them. But I name no persons, but leave the matter to God and their own consciences, desiring they may repent and make restitution.

From this time forward, our Christian Indian soldiers were constantly employed in all expeditions against the enemy, while the war lasted; and after the arrival of the ships from England, which was in May, arms were bought to furnish the rest of the able men; and then Capt. Hunting's company was made up to the number of eighty men; those did many signal services in the summer, 1676. At Weshakum, and at or near Mendon,

* For an interesting account of the Sudbury battle, see "Letters to London," (republished by Mr. Drake.)

at Mount Hope, at Watchusett, and several other places,* they were often made use of as scouts before the army, and at such time when the army lay still and staid at their quarters; in which scoutings they took several captives, and slew many of the enemy, and brought their scalps to their commanders. The particulars of their actions are too many to mention in this script. I contend that the small company of our Indian friends have taken and slain of the enemy, in the summer of 1676, not less than four hundred; and their fidelity and courage is testified by the certificates of their captains, that are inserted in the close of this discourse. It may be said in truth, that God made use of these poor, despised, and hated Christians, to do great service for the churches of Christ in New England, in this day of their trial; and I think it was observed by impartial men, that, after our Indians went out, the balance turned of the English side;. for, after the attack of Sudbury (at which time our Indians first went forth), the enemy went down the wind amain; and, about July, one hundred and fifty surrendered themselves to mercy to the Massachusetts government, besides several that surrendered at Plymouth and Connecticut. Among those that came in to Massachusetts with the sachem † of Packachooge,‡ there were several of those that had been praying Indians, and went or were carried away from Hassanamesit; of which I have before spoken.

About the 9th of August, there happened a very sad accident, relating to the poor Christian Indians, viz. a horrid murder committed by some Englishmen upon two squaws, wives to two of our Indian soldiers, the one named Andrew Pittimee, the captain of the Indians; and the other his sister (wife to one Thomas Speene §); and one young woman, and three children, whereof one was a nursing infant; and all the children of Thomas Speen aforesaid. These two squaws and their company aforementioned, being allowed (in this time of their straits for food) by the English authority, went forth to gather hurtleberries, at a place called Hurtleberry Hill, about four miles from Waterton mill, within the bounds of that town; where the English, who were about eleven or twelve in number, and were

---

* Of which Dedham was one. † Sagamore John.
‡ Partly in Worcester and partly in Ward.
§ For particulars respecting the families of Speen, see Biglow's *History of Natick* and *The Book of the Indians.*

on horseback, first met those Indians. There was one Indian
man with them, called John Stoolemester, one that had been
bred with the English; they disarmed him of a carbine belonging to the county, for he was newly come in from the army,
and had not delivered his arms. After they had disarmed this
fellow, they threatened to kill him; but he, speaking English,
interceded strongly for his life, and so they dismissed him, and
he came home; but the squaws being among the bushes not
far off, he lost them there; the English came to them and sat
down, and smok'd it where they were, and exchanged with
them bread and cheese for some hurtleberries; and then the
English left the squaws and children, but being not gone a mile,
four of the English left their company and went back to the
squaws, and drove them before them unto the north end of the
hill, into a secret place, and there murdered them all, and stript
such as had coats on. Having committed the murder, these
men went to their habitations. The next day after the squaws
were missing, and came not home to their wigwams, Capt. Pitimee, being then at home, came to Major Gookin at Cambridge
and acquainted him with his fears, that some evil had befallen
his wife, sister, and their company, and desired an order and
some help of Englishmen, two or three at least, to go and
search for them; which being so reasonable a request, it was
granted. So he went forth and searched a day or two, but could
not find them; at last, having procured about fifteen or sixteen
Indians and two English, they made a more strict search, and
at last found the dead bodies, not far from one another, cruelly
murdered, some shot through, others their brains beat out with
hatchets; to be short, this murder was afterward discovered,
and the four murderers seized, tried, and condemned, and two
of the four executed, and the other two pardoned by the General Court. This murder was very much decried by all good
men, and it was some satisfaction that some of them were made
examples. I know the murderers pretended a law to warrant
the act, but the juries and judge were not of their mind in the
matter. I know, also, there are some among the English, that
have a very ill conceit of all the Indians, and will not admit
them so much charity, as to think that any of them are sober or
honest; such I shall leave to the Lord, desiring he will give them
more charity, and root out of their hearts the spirit of enmity
and animosity. And it is probable that some persons will not be
wanting to calumniate our Christian Indians, and object that,

notwithstanding all that hath been said on their behalf, yet they are hypocrites and wicked men, and will frequently drink and commit other lewdness. To this I shall answer in few words.

I have good ground to believe, that several of them are sincere ; but I do not say they are all such. And I dare not affirm for my own countrymen, that there are no hypocrites or evil-doers among them. I wish and pray, that both English and Indians were all better than I fear they are; 't is not my work to judge men's hearts; that belongs to God. Secondly, I cannot deny but that many of them, especially the younger sort, that have been and are soldiers, but they are too apt to be overtaken with drink. I could wish they had not so much example and temptation thereunto by some English, especially such as have been their fellow-soldiers in the wars, who are very ready, when they meet the Indians, to give or procure strong drink for them; and others, for filthy lucre's sake, sell them strong drink, expressly prohibited by law; indeed, a very little matter will intoxicate their brains; for, being used to drink water, they cannot bear a fourth part of what an Englishman will bear. I have known one drunk with as little as one eighth part of a pint of strong water, and others with little more than a pint of cider. I do not plead to justify them in such actions, but endeavour to declare things as they are in truth. Thirdly, I cannot deny but sundry of the Christian Indians are not of so good conversation, as Christian religion requires; which thing is matter of lamentation to all that fear God, not only in respect of those Indians, but of the English also, among whom they live; yet, notwithstanding, we may not presently exclude them out of visible Christianity, but rather endeavour to convince and reform them, if God please to be instrumental to correct them, and turn them to God effectually. Whilst men do externally attend the means of grace, keep the Sabbath, pray in their families morning and evening, and endeavour and desire to be instructed in Christian religion, both themselves and children, as the praying Indians do, there is charitable encouragement and good hope, through grace, that, as God hath wrought effectually upon some, so he will upon others, in his own time and according to his good pleasure, that he hath purposed in himself. I account it my duty not to censure and judge, but to pray for them and others.

About the latter end of August, 1676, an army was sent against the eastern enemies, with whom Capt. Hunting and his company of Indians went, but this army did little against the enemy; but that which was done, was done by our Indians, who slew two or three of the enemy, but lost none of their lives, through God's favor.

Again on February 5th, 1676,* in another expedition to the eastern part, commanded by Major Waldron, wherein our praying Indians under Capt. Hunting bore a part, and some few of the enemy were killed by them; but their counsel was not attended in that expedition, which if it had been, as I heard some English in the service say, in probability the enemy had been greatly worsted at that time. In June, 1677, another expedition into the eastern parts, among whom were about thirty-six of our Christian Indians, who in a fight near Black Point, the English lost about forty men, whereof were eight of our friendly Indians, and their Lieutenant, James Richardson, was then slain; this was the greatest loss that our Indians sustained all the war; for in all the former expeditions our Indians lost but two men.

But I shall pass from this matter, and also from any further discourse of the military actions of our praying Indians, who to this day, upon all occasions of scouting in the woods, or any other hazardous services, are frequently employed as occasion doth present. Now I shall draw towards a close, only mention some few things concerning those of our Christian Indians, that have not been employed in the war, being not capable thereof; some by reason of age, and far the greatest part being women and children. But yet for religion, these, far the greater part of the religious, staid at home.

When their able men were for the generality drawn forth to the wars, the rest, being nearly four hundred old men, women, and children, were left upon Long Island, in a suffering state. It was intended they should plant corn upon the Islands, and in order thereunto they made some preparations, expending their labor upon clearing and breaking up ground; but some English, that lived on those Islands, and had interest there, were unfriendly to them, and discouraged them. But the authority of the country did interpose for their quiet; yet the poor Indians were discouraged, and in want of all things almost, except clams, which food (as some con-

---

* Old style must be understood; according to which the new year did not begin until 25th March.

ceived) did occasion fluxes and other diseases among them; besides, they were very mean for clothing, and the Islands were bleak and cold with the sea winds in spring time, and the place afforded little fuel, and their wigwams were mean. In this condition of want and sickness they were, after their men were sent for to the wars, until mid May; then God was pleased to mollify the hearts and minds of men towards them, by little and little; partly by the true reports brought to the General Court, of their distressed estate, and the great unlikelihood they were to plant or reap any corn at the Islands; and partly from the success God was pleased to give their brethren, abroad in the country's service; insomuch that the hearts of many were in a degree changed to those Christian Indians; and the General Court then sitting passed an order, giving liberty to remove them from the Islands, cautioning their order, that it should be done without charge to the country. This liberty being given, Major Gookin, their old friend and ruler, by the authority and encouragement of the Right Honorable the Corporation for Gospelizing the Indians, residing in London, and by authority of the General Court of Massachusetts in New England, forthwith hired boats to bring them from the Islands to Cambridge, not far from the house of Mr. Thomas Oliver, a pious man, and of a very loving, compassionate spirit to those poor Indians; who, when others were shy, he freely offered a place for their present settlement upon his land, which was very commodious for situation, being near Charles river, convenient for fishing, and where was plenty of fuel; and Mr. Oliver had a good fortification at his house, near the place where the wigwams stood, where (if need were) they might retreat for their security. This deliverance from the Island was a jubilee to those poor creatures; and though many of them were sick at this time of their removal, especially some of the chief men, as Waban, John Thomas, and Josiah Harding, with divers other men, women, and children, were sick of a dysentery and fever, at their first coming up from the Island; but by the care of the Major, and his wife, and Mr. Elliot, making provision for them, of food and medicines, several of them recovered, particularly Waban and John Thomas; the one the principal ruler, and the other a principal teacher of them, who were both extreme low, but God had in mercy raised them up; had they died it would have been a great weakening to the work of God

among them. The most of the Indians continued at this
place all the summer, some few excepted, that scattered
to places adjacent, to work for the English in harvest time.
But toward October they removed; some to the falls of
Charles river, and some settled about Hoanantum Hill; not
far from Mr. Oliver's, near the very place where they first
began to pray to God, and Mr. Elliot first taught them, which
was about thirty years since. Here Anthony, one of the
teachers, built a large wigwam, at which place the lecture
and the school were kept, in the winter 1676; where Major
Gookin and Mr. Elliot ordinarily met every fortnight; and
the other week among the Packemitt* Indians, who were
also brought from the Island at the same time, and placed near
Brush Hill,† in Milton, under the care of Quarter-master
Thomas Swift. This last summer, though they came up late
from the Island, yet they planted some ground, procured
for them by the Major among the English; and so they got
some little corn, and more for work; and their soldiers, that
were abroad, had corn provided by the country for their
relations; so that through God's favor they were pretty well
supplied. And in the winter time, about December, there was
abundance of a sort of fish called frost-fish, which they took
with scoop nets and dried great plenty of them. The widows
and the aged had supply of clothing and corn at the charge
of the Honorable Corporation in London, who tenderly and
compassionately ordered relief for such as were in need; and
many of the men, who were about home, got plenty of venison
in the winter 1676, for supply of their families, so that God
provided for their outward subsistence. And for religion, I
hope it begins to revive among them. There were seven
places where they met to worship God and keep the Sabbath, viz. at Nonatum,‡ at Packemit or Punkapog, at Cowate *alias* the fall of Charles river, at Natick, at Medfield,
at Concord, and at Namkeake, near Chelmsford; in which
places there was at each place a teacher and schools for
the youth at most of them. Mr. Elliot kept his lecture
weekly, at Nonantum and Pakomit, where also Major Gookin kept his courts among them. When the winter was
over, 1676, and the spring drew on, the praying Indians most

---

* Or Punkapog, since Stoughton.   † Still known by the same name.
‡ Before written by the author *Hoanantum.* Hutchinson, I. 163,
has *Noonanetum.*

of them repaired to their plantations at Natick, Magunkog, and some planted at Hassanamesit; but not long after, they withdrew from thence and gave over tending their corn, for fear of the Maquas, who had been among Unkas' men, and done some mischief and carried away one of Unkas' sons prisoners, but he was again released by them. Some of the praying Indians planted among the English plantations, as at Medfield, Concord, Cambridge, and Chelmsford, and got supplies by their labor. Before they removed from Cowate, there was a poor widow woman of the praying Indians, that went to gather some flags to make mats, about two or three miles. She being alone, and her company gone before her, home, was met by an Englishman of Sudbury, named Curtis, who required her to go with him; she being unwilling, made way to escape from him homeward to the wigwams, but he outran her, and with his hatchet helve he wounded her very sore in several places about the head, leaving her all in her blood; but she being, not mortally wounded (as it proved), made a shift to get to the wigwams, where she lay by a long time, before she recovered. She knew not who it was that had offered her this injury; but the man spake of it himself, and pretended the woman beat him, and what he did was in his own defence. It is probable she struggled what she could when he was beating her.

In the summer, 1677,* several of our Indian soldiers were employed; some to scout with Lieut. Richardson upon the borders of Merrimack, to watch the motions of the eastern enemy; others were sent to keep garrison in the east parts, as Cocheco, York, Wells, and Black Point; others were sent with a small army to Black Point, where eight of them were slain, as is before hinted. In September, the Mahawks or Maquas (contrary to their promises and agreement) came down in small parties among our praying Indians, and put them into great trouble. A party of the Maquas took two widow women captives, being at Hassanamesit (one of their plantations) to make or fetch cider. The same party of Mahawks, or another party, came down within half a mile of an English house belonging to Sudbury, and murdered a very honest Indian, named Josiah

* We have no particulars of this affair; and, according to Williamson, *History of Maine.* I. 552, a treaty had been made in August before, and it would seem, that all was now tranquil.

Nowell,* who was going to his   This man had a wife
and four small children. His brother-in-law, James Speen, (a
very pious man,) parted from him not half an hour before he
was slain, appointing to meet him at a place designated; but
the other came not, and his brother hallooed for him; yet,
notwithstanding, the Maquas met not this man, but God preserved him. The English sent forth to pursue this Maquas,
with some other Indians, but they could not overtake them.
But the Maquas carried the captives through Hadley, some
few days after, and showed the scalp of the man slain to the
English at Hadley;† who would willingly have redeemed the
squaws, but could not prevail with the Maquas to let them go.
About this time, viz. in September, 1677, our praying Indians,
that lived at Natick, built up their forts and the like, which
they did at Pakemit. In this month of September, about the
19th day, a party of Indians fell upon a village called Hatfield,
near Hadley; they burnt some dwelling-houses and barns, that
stood without the line, and wounded and killed about twelve
persons, and carried away captive twenty English persons, most
of them women and children.‡ It was conceived, at first, that
this mischief was done by a party of Mawhakes, because it was
done the next day after the Maquas, with the two Indian captives before spoken of, were carried through the town of Hadley. But it appeared afterward, by an English prisoner that
escaped from the enemy, that this party of Indians were about
twenty-seven in all, whereof four were women; who were of
the old enemy, and formerly neighbours; who had fled to the
French about Quebec, and were lately come from thence with
the company of another ply of Indians, who were gone toward
Merrimack; for, on the very same day, another ply of Indians,
that came from the French, came to Naamkeke, near Chelmsford; and there, either by force or persuasion, carried away
with them Wannalancet, the sachem, and all his company, excepting two men, whereof one was the minister, and their wives
and children, and one widow that escaped to the English.

---

* The Mohawks had been urged by agents, sent by the authorities of
Massachusetts, to come down upon the New England Indians. This
murder was probably among the first fruits of that misguided policy.

† "The lands bordering on Connecticut river, which are now in the
towns of Northampton, Hadley, and Hatfield, were first known by the
Indian name *Nonotuck.*" — Williams's *Sketch of Northampton,* p. 6.

‡ See Hubbard's *History of New England,* p. 636.

Those that went away were about fifty, whereof there were not above eight men, the rest women and children; and we never heard more of them since. It was a matter of scandal and offence, (to such as are ready to take up any thing to reproach the profession of religion among the Indians,) that this man, Wannalancet, who made a profession of religion, should thus go away, when he was reconciled to the English and well esteemed generally by them, and had no cause given him for it. But forasmuch as there may be some reasons given for this man's acting thus at this time, that may tend to excuse him, of which I have certain knowledge, I shall here briefly mention them. First, this man had but a weak company, not above eight men; and those, except two or three, unarmed. Secondly, he lived at a dangerous frontier place, both for the Maquas, that were now in small parties watching opportunities to slay and captivate these Indians, and had lately done mischief a few miles off, as is before mentioned; on the other side, the eastern Indians, that were in hostility with the English, might easily have access to this place. Thirdly, he had but little corn to live on for the ensuing winter, for his land was improved by the English before he came in. Fourthly, the Indians that came from the French were his kindred and relations, for one of them was his wife's brother; and his eldest son also lived with the French. Fifthly, those Indians informed him, that the war was not yet at an end, and that he would live better and with more safety among the French; who, in truth, do much indulge the Indians, and furnish them whatever they desire, because they employ those Indians to kill them beaver, and moose, and other peltry, whereby they gain much. These and other reasons did, in probability, so far prevail to persuade him, which, together with the force they had to compel him, in case he refused, so that he went away with them. But they went off quietly, and did no mischief in the least to the English, which I rationally impute to Wannalancet's being with them; for he was a person not of a mischievous or bloody disposition, but of a prudent and peaceable spirit, and, it is like, was unwilling (so far as he could prevent it) that the English should receive any injury, or have any just cause of offence, at this time of his leaving them; because it is not impossible he may, in convenient time, return again to live with the English in his own country, and upon his own land; which (as I have observed) the Indians do much incline unto.

At a Court held among the praying Indians, where was a
full meeting of them, it being also Mr. Elliot's lecture, who was
present with Major Gookin and some other English, Waban,
the chief ruler among the Indians, in the name of all the rest,
made an affectionate speech to this effect: "We do, with all
thankfulness, acknowledge God's great goodness to us, in preserving us alive to this day. Formerly, in our beginning to
pray unto God, we received much encouragement from many
godly English, both here and in England. Since the war
begun between the English and wicked Indians, we expected
to be all cut off, not only by the enemy Indians, whom we
know hated us, but also by many English, who were much
exasperated and very angry with us. In this case, we cried
to God, in prayer, for help. Then God stirred up the governor and magistrates to send us to the Island, which was grievous
to us; for we were forced to leave all our substance behind us,
and we expected nothing else at the Island, but famine and
nakedness. But behold God's goodness to us and our poor
families, in stirring up the hearts of many godly persons in
England, who never saw us, yet showed us kindness and much
love, and gave us some corn and clothing, together with other
provision of clams, that God provided for us. Also, in due
time, God stirred up the hearts of the governor and magistrates, to call forth some of our brethren to go forth to fight
against the enemy both to us and the English, and was pleased to give them courage and success in that service, unto the
acceptance of the English; for it was always in our hearts to
endeavour to do all we could. to demonstrate our fidelity to
God and to the English, and against their and our enemy; and
for all these things, we desire God only may be glorified."
Piambow,* the other ruler next to Waban, spake to the same,
giving all glory to the Lord. After this, upon occasion of an
inquiry concerning the messengers sent, in winter last, to Mohegan, to stir the Mohegans up to pray to God, some English
reported, that those messengers enticed some of the Indian servants, at Norwich, to run away with those messengers, from
their masters; but the messengers utterly denied any such
thing. Waban took this occasion, further to speak to this
effect: "That God knew, that they had done their utmost endeavours to carry themselves so that they might approve their

---

* Otherwise written *Piam Boohan.*

fidelity and love to the English. But yet, some English were still ready to speak the contrary of them, as in this matter instanced; and in that business at Cocheco, lately, when the Indians were carried away by the Maquas; yet the English say, they ran away to the Maquas and were not carried away; yet," said he, " I know the governor and magistrates and many good men had other thoughts of them and more charity toward them." To this speech of his, Major Gookin made this answer: " That Christ in the Gospel teacheth all his disciples to take up the cross daily. And he himself, though most innocent, and always did good, yet some said of him, he had a devil; others, that he was an enemy to Cesar; others, that he was a friend to publicans and sinners, and raised many other reproaches against him; yet he bore all patiently, and referred the case to God; and herein we should follow his example. Waban, you know all Indians are not good; some carry it rudely, some are drunkards, others steal, others lie and break their promises, and otherwise wicked. So 't is with Englishmen; all are not good, but some are bad, and will carry it rudely; and this we must expect, while we are in this world; therefore, let us be patient and quiet, and leave this case to God, and wait upon him in a way of well-doing, patience, meekness, and humility; and God will bring a good issue in the end, as you have seen and experienced."

There are many other things, that I might have recorded, concerning these poor, despised sheep of Christ. But I fear that which I have already written will be thought (by some) impertinent and tedious. But when I call to mind, that great and worthy men have taken much pains to record, and others to read, the seeming small and little concerns of the children of God; as well in the historical books of Scripture, as other histories of the primitive times of Christianity, and of the doings and sufferings of the poor saints of God; I do encourage my heart in God, that He will accept, in Christ, this mean labor of mine, touching these poor despised men; yet such as are, through the grace of Christ, the first professors, confessors, if I may not say martyrs, of the Christian religion among the poor Indians in America.

FINIS.

CERTIFICATES.

Major Thomas Savage his Certificate concerning the Praying Indians.

THESE do certify, that I, Thomas Savage, of Boston, being commander of the English forces at Mount Hope, in the beginning of the war between the English and Indians, about July, 1675, and afterward in March, 1676, at Menumesse and Hadley. In both which expeditions, some of the Christian Indians belonging to Natick, &c., were in the army; as at Mount Hope, were about forty men, and at Menumesse six men. I do testify, on their behalf, that they carried themselves well, and approved themselves courageous soldiers, and faithful to the English interest.

Dated at Boston, the 20th day of December, 1677.

THOMAS SAVAGE.

Captain Daniel Henchman's Certificate concerning the Praying Indian Soldiers.

These may certify, that I, Daniel Henchman, of Boston, being appointed and authorized by the Governor and Council of Massachusetts, not only to look unto and order the praying Indians, for some part of the time that they were confined to Deer Island; but, likewise, to have the command of several of them as soldiers, both at Mount Hope, in the beginning of the war, 1675; and also in another expedition, May and June, 1676, when I had the command of the English forces at Weshakum, Mendon, and Hadley; in all which time I had experience of the sobriety, courage, and fidelity of the generality of those Indians. And this I do testify, under my hand, and could say much more on their behalf, if time and opportunity permitted.

Dated at Boston, this 29th of November, 1677.

D. HENCHMAN.

Captain Samuel Hunting's Certificate about the Christian Indian Soldiers.

These are to certify, that I, Samuel Hunting, of Charlestown, in New England, being, by authority of the Governor and Council, appointed commander of the praying Indians living in the Massachusetts colony, in New England, in the war against the barbarous Indians; did accordingly command the said Indian company, consisting (when at the most) of not above eighty men. The said company, with myself, served the country, in several expeditions, for about one year's time. In all which service, the said Indians behaved themselves courageously and faithfully to the English interest; and I conceive, that the said company did kill and take prisoners above two hundred of the enemy, and lost but one man of ours; besides about one hundred persons they killed and took prisoners at other times, when I was not with them, and they went out volunteers. And, in testimony of the truth hereof, I have hereunto set my hand, this 13th day of December, 1677.

SAMUEL HUNTING.

DOCUMENTS

GOOKIN'S HISTORY OF THE CHRISTIAN INDIANS.

No. I. — See page 476.

To the Honourable the Govournour and Councill of the Massachusetts Colony, Assembled at Boston this   of June 1676:

THE humble petition of Andrew Pittimee, Quanahpohkit, *alias* James Rumney Marsh, John Magus, and James Speen, officers unto the Indian souldiers, now in your service, with the consent of the rest of the Indian souldiers being about eighty men;

Humbly imploreth your favour and mercies to be extended to some of the prisoners taken by us, (most of them) near Lanchaster, Marlborough, &c: In whose behalf we are bold to supplicate your Honoures. And wee have three reasons for this our humble supplication; first, because the persons we beg pardon for, as we are informed, are innocent; and have not done any wrong or injury unto the English, all this war time, only were against their wills, taken and kept among the enemy. Secondly, because it pleased your Honours to say to some of us, to encourage us to fidelity and activity in your service, that you would be ready to do any thing for us, that was fitt for us to ask and you to grant. Thirdly, that others that are out, and love the English, may be encouraged to come in. More that we humbly intercede for, is the lives and libertyes of those few of our poor friends and kindred, that, in this time of temptation and affliction, have been in the enemy's quarters; we hope it will be no griefe of heart to you to shew mercy, and especially to such who have (as we conceive) done no wrong to the English. If wee did think, or had any ground to conceive that they were naught, and were enemies to the English, we would not intercede for them, but rather bear our testimony against them, as we have done. We have (especially some of us) been sundry times in your service to the hazzard of our lives, both as spyes, messengers, scouts, and souldiers, and have through God's favour acquitted ourselves faithfully, and shall do as long as we live endeavour with all fidelitie to fight in the English cause, which we judge is our own cause, and also God's cause, to oppose the wicked Indians, enemies to God and all goodness. In granting this our humble request, you will much oblige us who desire to to remain

Your Honoures Humble and Faithful Servants,

> ANDREW PITTIMEE,
> JAMES QUANAPOHKIT,
> JOB,
> JOHN MAGUS,
> JAMES SPEEN.

The persons we supplicate for, are Capt. Tom, his son Nehemiah, his wife and two children, John Uktuek, his wife and children, Maanum and her child.

And if the Councill please not to answer our desires in granting the lives and liberties of all these, yett if you shall please to grant us the women and children, it will be a favour unto us.

In answer to the Petition of James Quanhpohkit, James Speen, Job, Andrew Pittimee, and Jno. Magus.

CAPT. TOM being a lawful prisoner at warr, there needs no further evidence for his conviction ; yet hee having had liberty to present his plea before the Councill why he should not be proceeded against accordingly, instead of presenting any thing that might alleviate his withdrawing from the government of the English and joyning with the enemy, it doth appear by sufficient evidence that hee was not only (as is credibly related by some Indians present with him) an instigator to others over whom he was by this government made a Captain, but also was actually present and an actor in the devastation of some of our plantations ; and therefore it cannot consist with the honour and justice of authority to grant him a pardon.

Whereas the Council do, with reference to the faithful service of the Petitioners, grant them the lives of the women and children by them mentioned. And, further, the Councill do hereby declair, that, as they shall be ready to show favour in sparing the lives and liberty of those that have been our enemys, on their comeing in and submission of themselves to the English Government and your disposal, the reality and complacency of the government towards the Indians sufficiently appearing in the provisions they have made, and tranquility that the Pequots have injoyed under them for over forty years; so also it will not be availeable for any to plead in favour for them that they have been our friends while found and taken among our enemyes.

Further the Councill do hereby declare that none may expect priviledge bye his declaration, that come not in and submit themselves in 14 days next coming.

By the Council,   EDW. RAWSON, *Clerke.*

***

No. II. — See page 484.

For the Honourable the Gouernor and Councill of Massachu-setts Colony, in New England.

May it please your Honours,

I am bold at the intreaty of the wife of John Hoare, of Concord, to intercede with your honours, on the behalfe of herselfe and husband. (who posibly, upon some consideration, may deserve no great favours of you,) yet I presume upon arguements of justise and righteousnes; you will have no respect to persons, but doe that which is equall and right. It is upon this account that I move in this case.

It pleased your honours to appoint Major Willard, Mr. Eliot, and myselfe, as your comittee, to ride up to Concord and Chelmsford, about the middle of December last, to endeavour the settlement of the Nashobah Indians, (then at Concord,) under such care and conduct as might quiet and compose men's minds in those parts, at that juncture; yourselves finding, at that time, a great difficulty in that matter, because the Natick and Punkapog Indians being then at the Island, when they were attended with straits for fuelle and victulls, you were not willing to send more thither; now there was no man in Concord appered willing to take care of and secure those Indians, but Mr. John Hoare, whome the Counsill accepted and approved;

and at that time, I remember, Mr. Hoare moved for two things: first, that hee and his family might bee free from impressment, and that the country rates, due at that time, should bee abated him; to which, as I apprehended, yourselves conceded; and when wee made a more particular settlement and conclusion of the matter at Concord, hee spake of the same matter, to which the Comittee answered, they aprehended that the Councill would not faile of their promise.   This I know, that Mr. Hoare lay'd out a very considerable matter for the accommodating of the affaire, I beelieve five times as much as his rates, which is wholy lost to him; indeed, had the Indians beene continued with him, posibly they might have repayred his charge; but being taken from him after six or seven months cumber and care, hee lost much by it.   My humble and earnest request is, that the first payment of eight rates, due when hee had the Indians under his care, may be remitted to his wife.   This, I conceive, will not bee aboue three or four pounds.   If you please to grant this, my request, I conceive you will doe a righteous act, and will obleige your seruant, to bee ready to serve you and the country, when   made in your name and in order to your service and the countries, shall be accomplished.

So, with my humble servise presented,
I rest your humble servant,
DANIEL GOOKIN, Sen.

Cambridge, 30th of Nouember, 1676.

No. III. — See page 497.

To the Honoured Governor and Councill assembled at Boston, this 14th of January, 1675.

JOHN HOAR humbly sheweth,

That whereas, on a motion made by myself, by order of Major Willard, about the Nashoby Indians, viz. That they now do eat their own bread, which they are still content to do. 2. To help what they are capable to do, about building of an house sutable for to teach them in manufactures, which also they are still willing to do according to their abillities; which is, by the delay of not concluding the busines before winter, £30 damage to them and me, which I forbear to relate.   3. That I, and my family employed therein, should be freed from publique charges, and also from publique service during this employ. Now the committee, as you see by their order here inclosed, they have engaged me to see that they do receive no damage to, or prejudice from the English. For the Indians doing no prejudice to the English, I hope I shall accomplish to your honours' satisfaction, with the rest of what is desired respecting me, only they say that they are under my conduct and ordering. Now I humbly move to know your honours' pleasure, whether you will be pleased to give us leave to make our own orders, both for regulating our affaires and punishing offenders; which, being ratified by yourselves or your committee, may be our lawfull power in all proceedings. Or whether you or your committee will give us orders sutable to our society. As also, what way I shall be directed to save the Indians from the insolency of the English, being daily threatned to be shott, and one snapt at thrice at my own dore by a Lankastsheir souldier; or whether, you will likewise give me leave to propose to you, what I conceive may be a suitable remedy, which I deem can no wise be offensive or prejudiciall to any that own themselves subject to the lawes of this Government. I shall wait for your answer, still praying that all under you may live a peaceable life, in all godliness and honesty. As in duty bound,

Your humble servant to be commanded,

JOHN HOAR.

In answer to this petition, the Councill do herby exempt John Hoare and his family, from being impressed into the country service, during such time as hee is employed in looking to the Indians. Secondly, as for exemption from publike charges, the Councill do not grant it; but reffer it to the Generall Court, to whome hee may apply himselfe; but if the petitioner, upon expense, do acquit himselfe so in that imploy, as the court shall see benefitt accrue to the publike by it, they conceiv the court will consider the petitioner some other way, for his incouragement. Thirdly, if the petitioner have any thing further to offer to the Councill or court, for the publik weale and good of the Indians, the Councill shall be willing to heare it, and give such answer as shall be agreeable to reason. 15th January, 1675.

Past.   EDW. RAWSON, *Secretary.*

No. IV — See page 518.

1676, November 10th — An account of the disposall of the Indians, our freinds (pro tempore), presented to the Council (at their desire) by Daniel Gookin, sen.

The Punkapog Indians are residing about Milton, Dorchester, and Brantree, among the English, who employ them (as I am informed) to cut cord wood, and do other labors. These are under the inspection of quarter-master Thomas Swift; their number, as I conjecture, may bee about one hundred and seventy-five; whereof   35 men : 140 women and children.

The Naticke Indians are disposed in fower companies, as followese, vict: one company, with James Rumny Marsh and his kindred, live in Meadfield, with the approbation and consent of the English; these are in number about twenty-five. 5 : 20.

Another company live neare Natick, adjoyning to the garrison-house of Andrew Dewin and his sons, (who desire their neighbourhood,) and are under their inspection; the number of these may be about fifty souls.   10 : 40.

A third company of them, with Waban, live neare the falls of Charles river, neare to the house of Joseph Miller, and not farr from Capt. Prentce. The number of these may be about sixty souls; whereof are   12 : 50.

A fourth company dwell at Noantum-hill, neare Leift. Trowbridge and John Coones, who permitts them to build their wigwams upon his ground. The number of this company, including some yt live neare John White's, of Mudy river, and a family or two neare Mr. Sparhake, and Daniel Champney, and Mr. Thomas Olivers, which are employed by the said persons to cut wood, and spin, and make stone walls; being but a small distance from the hill of Nonatum, where their meeting is to keepe Sabath. These may bee about seventy-five souls.
                                        15 : 60.

☞ Among the Natick Indians are to bee reckned such as are left, which came in with John of Pakchoog; which are not many, for sundry of that company are dead (since they came in); above thirty are put out to seruice to the English; three were executed about Tho. Eames his burning; about twenty rann away; and, generally, such as remaine are of those Indians yt formerly (before the war) lived under our government at Hassanamesit, Magunkog, Marlborouh, and Wamesitt. The men belonging to these are not above fifteen, and they are abroad with the army at the eastward, under Capt. Hunting.

The Nashobah or Concord Indians live at Concord, with the consent of the English there, and are employed by ym; and are under the inspection of the comittee of militia and selectmen of yt towne. Their number may be about fifty.

10 : 40.

The Indians that relate to Wannalancet, are placed neare Mr. Jonathan Ting's, at Dunstable, with Mr. Tyng's consent and under his inspection (when at home); and in Mr. Tyng's absence, the care of them is under one Robert Parris, Mr. Tyng's bayl. The number of these may be about sixty, or more; some of their children are ordered to be put forth to English service, by the selectmen of Chelmsford and comittee of militia there.

10 : 50.

There are about twenty-five live at or about Ipswich, under the gouernment of authority there; som of yr children were ordered to be put to service; there are about twenty-five.

8 : 17.

Besides these, there are some familys of ym yt live about Watertown and in Cambridge bounds, under English inspection and neare ym; as at one Gate's, at Watertown, two familes; at Justinias Holden, one family; at or neare Corprall Humand, two familys; at one Wilson, at Shawshin, one family. All these may be about forty souls.

7 : 33.

117 men, 450 women and children; and in all 567.

☞It must not be understood, that this compution of ye number is exact; they may be a few more or a few less. Also, of the men there are above thirty now abroad, under Capt. Hunting, at the eastward.

All these Indians meet together to worship God and keepe the Sabath; and have their teachers at six places, viz.: Meadfield, Andrew Dewins, at Lower Falls, at Nonnanum, at Concord, at Dunstable.

Mr. Hull,

The Pankapoog Indians, and particularly John Hunt comes to me (as hee saith from the Councel) to demand their wages for service done the country. Their demand is reasonable and just for ought I know. But if it bee expected that I should recken with them and the other Indian souldiers; there are seuerall things must bee done by yourselfe and the Councill before I am capable to effect it, or audit their acc'ts, as

1. I must have due certificate of the time that they have been in the service.

2. An acc't of all the Comissaries, as at Concord, Dedham, Hadly, Marlborow, and of Corporall Swift or others, what goods, mony, corn, or other things they have rece'd, for they are apt to bee receving every where.

3. I must bee furnished with mony and goods to satisfy them. Most things that were sent to Cambridge, are delivered already, exept som drawers, calico shirts, and shooes, and a small remnant of cotton; and about 20s. in mony.

4. It must be determined what wages they must have, and whether any that are called officers among them shall be allowed more than the private soldier.

5. It must bee determined whether your demand for scalps they have brought in, and prisoners they have taken, shall be allowed one coat for a scalpe, and two coats for a prisoner.

These things must bee answered, and resolved, and supplied, before I can possibly auditt your acc'ts, or pass your debenters; which I thinke should bee don with all the convenient speed may bee, for they are in a needy condition, and their harts are upon their wages; and yet I conceive when they come to reckon, many of them will be found to have receaved most of their dues allready. I pray, Sir, please to impart this my letter to the Counsel and send me an answer about it, that I may satisfy the Indians, and not put them off with delayes.

So with my due respects presented to you, I rest

Your assured freind and servant,

DANIEL GOOKIN, Sen.

Cambridg, August 14th,
1676.

CPSIA information can be obtained
at www.ICGtesting.com
Printed in the USA
BVHW050108290820
587363BV00006B/270